Excellence
in
Upper-Level Writing
2018/2019

**The Gayle Morris
Sweetland Center for Writing**

Edited by
Dana Nichols

Published in 2019 by Michigan Publishing
University of Michigan Library

© 2019 Gayle Morris Sweetland Center for Writing

Permission is required to reproduce material from this title in other
publications, coursepacks, electronic products, and other media.

Please send permission requests to:

Michigan Publishing
1210 Buhr Building
839 Greene Street
Ann Arbor, MI 48104
lib.pod@umich.edu

ISBN 978-1-60785-546-0

Table of Contents
Excellence in Upper-Level Writing

Winners list 5

Nominees list 6

Introduction 7

Prize for Excellence in Upper-Level Writing

(Sciences)

Climate Change Exacerbates Invasive Species Pressures on 9
   Michigan Prairies

Current research on exoplanets and the search for habitable worlds 35

Prize for Excellence in Upper-Level Writing

(Social Sciences)

Best Strategies to Increase Public Support for a Tax on 53
   Sugar-Sweetened Beverages

Colonialism and Environmental Discrimination in the Asia-Pacific: 75
   The US military in Guam and Okinawa

Prize for Excellence in Upper-Level Writing

(Humanities)

Tinker, Tailor, Author, Masochist: The Ishiguro Novel as a Field 97
   Experiment in Pain

Bitchin' About the Kitchen: An Intersectional Review of Gender, Race, 111
   and Class in the Restaurant Industry

Excellence in Upper-Level Writing 2017/2018

Sweetland Writing Prize Chair

Dana Nichols

Sweetland Writing Prize Committee

Angie Berkley

Jimmy Brancho

Cat Cassel

Raymond McDaniel

Dana Nichols

Carol Tell

Sweetland Writing Prize Judges

Michelle Bellino

Katherine Beydler

Anne Gere

Katherine Hummel

Vincent Longo

Aleksandra Marciniak

Despina Margomenou

Raymond McDaniel

Elizabeth McNeill

Kamaria Porter

Emily Saidel

George Taylor

Administrative Support

Laura Schulyer

Aaron Valdez

Winners List

Excellence in Upper-Level Writing (Sciences)

Timothy Arvan, "Climate Change Exacerbates Invasive Species Pressures on Michigan Prairies" | *Nominated by Abby Potts, EEB372: Ecology Lab*

Elizabeth Stanley, "Current research on exoplanets and the search for habitable worlds" | *Nominated by Jimmy Brancho, Writing 400: Writing and Research in the Sciences*

Excellence in Upper-Level Writing (Social Sciences)

Samantha Goldstein, "Best Strategies to Increase Public Support for a Tax on Sugar-Sweetened Beverages" | *Nominated by Aloka Narayanan (GSI) and Nancy Burns (Faculty), PS 381: Introduction to Research Design*

Henry Schnaidt, "Colonialism and Environmental Discrimination in the Asia-Pacific: The US military in Guam and Okinawa" | *Nominated by Omolade Adunbi, AAS322/Environ 335: Introduction to Environmental Politics*

Excellence in Upper-Level Writing (Humanities)

Verity Sturm, "Tinker, Tailor, Author, Masochist: The Ishiguro Novel as a Field Experiment in Pain" | *Nominated by Andrea Zemgulys, English 398.002: Clones, Detectives, Artists, and a Shiny Nobel Prize (The Case of Ishiguro)*

Kelly Wester, "Bitchin' About the Kitchen: An Intersectional Review of Gender, Race, and Class in the Restaurant Industry" | *Nominated by Supriya Nair, English 407.002: Food and Culture*

Nominees List

Student	Instructor
Vinith Babu	Luis Mendez
Alexis Ball	Natasha Abner
Alayna Brasch	Julie Halpert
Hannah Chosid	Chalem Bolton
Meghan Clark	Christian de Pee
Dominique Cornitcher	Chalem Bolton
Natalie Cuevas	Jennifer Metsker
Arabella Delgado	Erik Mueggler
Noam Dovas	Gabriel VanLoozen
Sydney Edelstein	Supriya Nair
Fareah Fysudeen	Aric Knuth
Josh Greenberg	Sarah Buss
Erika Hammerstein	Michael Meyer
Sharif-Ahmed Krabti	Lucy Peterson
Suzanne Kaufman	Andrei Markovits
Jesse Kozler	Sarah Buss
Sophia Liu	Elizabeth Goodenough
Alexander Lopez	Jimmy Brancho
Rio Mizuno	Julie Halpert
Nicole Newman	Erik Mueggler
Kenneth O'Donnell	Abby Potts
Haoi An Pham	Colin Corrigan
Dylan Piacelli	Elyce Rotella
Ajilan Potter	Natasha Abner
Brittany Rivera	Luis Mendez
Danielle Sarns	Dylan Ellefson
Caryn Sherbet	Erin McAuliffe
Rachel Shutty	Erin McAuliffe
Emily Soong	Angela Kane
Amy Wensley	Angela Kane
Kennedy Werner	Molly Beer
Jason Wong	Jennifer Cummings
Elizabeth Wood	Molly Beer

Introduction

In an effort to assure that students who graduate from the College of Literature, Science and the Arts are effective writers, the College requires all students to complete a course that meets the upper level writing requirement. These courses are offered by approximately 35 departments every semester, and regardless of the department in which they appear, all these courses aim to help students build on their first-year writing courses in learning to write effectively within and beyond the disciplines they study; use feedback to revise their writing; and become familiar with the conventions and multiple genres of writing. The writing included in this volume represents some of the best selections produced by students in upper level writing courses during the past year.

The upper level writing requirement has existed since the late 1970s, and it was originally conceived as a means of preparing students to write effectively in their major areas of study. Students were expected to learn to write "like" an economist, a biologist, or whatever their major. These days the majority of students do not major in one field; they carry double majors or some combination of majors and minors. Accordingly, the upper level requirement has shifted its emphasis away for an entirely discipline-focused approach, recognizing that students may well not be fulfilling the requirement in their major or even one of their minors.

A recent study of students' development as writers shows that they adapt University and departmental requirements to fit their own purposes. They may choose a particular upper level writing course because it deals with a topic they want to learn about, because it compliments another course they have taken, because they want to continue working with a specific professor, or for any number of other reasons. Regardless of their reasons and regardless of the particular course they select, all students learn to address multiple audiences, to work productively with their peers in writing workshops that guide their revisions, and to use many different genres effectively, as the selections included here demonstrate.

Another development that has shaped upper level writing courses in recent years is the emergence of digital writing, writing that is enhanced by or "born" digital. Instructors, aware of the many ways students will be expected to write effectively with digital tools in the 21st century, frequent require students to produce video essays, podcasts, and electronic portfolios in writing courses, and Sweetland's upper level writing competition has begun to receive nominations in these formats. We expect the proportion of multimedia nominations to increase in coming years.

Whatever format students in upper level courses use, we expect the writing to be effective, convincing, and polished. As the selections included in this collection demonstrate, we have not been disappointed. Instructors nominated an impressive array of writing, and judges, including me, struggled to choose winners from among them because all were of such high quality. Each of the three divisions— social science, humanities, and natural science—included an impressive array. The judges for this competition were Michelle Bellino, Katherine Beydler, Anne Gere, Katherine Hummel, Vincent Longo, Aleksandra Marciniak, Despina Margomenou, Raymond McDaniel, Elizabeth McNeill, Kamaria Porter, Emily Saidel, and George Taylor. Much gratitude is owed to these judges and to Aaron Valdez, who designed this book; Laura Schuyler, who coordinated the submission process; and, especially, to Dana Nichols, who served as editor.

Anne Ruggles Gere, Director
Sweetland Center for Writing

Excellence in Upper-Level Writing (Sciences)

Climate Change Exacerbates Invasive Species Pressures on Michigan Prairies
by Timothy Arvan
From Course: EEB 372: Ecology Lab
Nominated by Abby Potts

Timothy received 100% on this essay. This research paper was the final culmination of a semester's worth of work. Timothy showed scientific excellence in the quality of his project, his worth ethic, attitude, and willingness to help classmates.

Abby Potts

Climate Change Exacerbates Invasive Species Pressures on Michigan Prairies

Abstract:

This study was motivated by the research question: how do invasive species and climate change pressures affect native plant biomass in Michigan prairies? Simulated heat stress and flooding episodes were administered to Michigan native Rudbeckia hirta populations facing simultaneous pressure from introduced invasive Centaurea maculosa. After a four-week growth period, R. hirta individuals were dehydrated and massed. Data suggest increasing climate change disturbances and invasive species pressures to each exert a statistically significant negative effect on native plant biomass. Importantly, a significant synergistic effect was also found under the combined influence of climate and invasive species stress, indicating the capacity for forecasted climate change to exacerbate extant strain on native plant systems. Results underline the urgency with which conservation techniques must be mobilized to facilitate climate change adaptation in prairie ecosystems.

Introduction:

Climate change increases the frequency and intensity of natural disturbances (i.e. heat waves, flooding, hurricanes, droughts, and wildfires), inflicting pervasive consequences on global ecological systems and human civilization (French, Robinson, & Lia, 2017). Environmental stresses induced by climate change place increasing burdens on native plant communities as plant populations face threats such as range shifts, pollinator extinctions, and invasive species (Diez et al., 2012) (Thuiller et al., 2008). These pressures inform the role of ecological research to guide development of innovative management approaches to ensure the long-term health of native plant systems. Indeed, without intensive study in this area, terrestrial communities will continue to face unmitigated biodiversity loss, reductions in the value of ecosystem services—such as agricultural productivity—essential to sustain human systems, and episodes of ecosystem collapse (Dukes et al., 2009).

In this study, Michigan native *Rudbeckia hirta* (black-eyed Susan) wildflower stands were experimentally colonized by increasing densities of invasive *Centaurea maculosa* (spotted knapweed) under concurrent simulated heat stress and flood episodes, mimicking forecasted near-term climate change-induced ecological change on Michigan prairies. Heightened precipitation levels and sustained elevated temperatures are among the climate change impacts most frequently cited as causal factors behind expected change in Michigan ecosystems in coming decades (Hellmann, Byers, Bierwagen, & Dukes, 2008). Furthermore, climate change has already been implicated in changing species compositions in Michigan forests (Hellmann, Byers, Bierwagen, & Dukes, 2008), while the latest National Climate Assessment report has implicated climate-induced loss of native flora as a central driver of midwestern pollinator declines. In light of climate change's imposition of significant forecasted losses in ecological, economic, and cultural value of Michigan ecosystems, continued analysis of regional vulnerabilities is necessary to guide the deployment of strategic interventions (Hayhoe, VanDorn, Croley, Schlegal, & Wuebbles). It is therefore the objective of this study's quantitative methodology to investigate the relationship between climate disturbances and invasive success by measuring native *R. hirta* mass after exposure to combined climate change and invasive species treatments.

Analysis of invasive species dynamics is an emerging sub-field of ecology integral to the deployment of effective conservation strategies in the face of climate change. In the context of this study, examination of parallel invasive plant literature in marine-coastal and desert contexts informed the hypothesis that *if* plant ecosystems are exposed to heightened temperature and precipitation pressures in disturbance events, *then* they will become more vulnerable to colonization by invasive species, *because* invasive species are generally more thermotolerant and accommodating of changes in soil moisture, lending them a competitive advantage in rapidly changing environments (Zerebecki & Sorte, 2011). This phenomenon was thus expected to produce a statistically significant negative interactive effect from invasive species presence and climate change pressures on native plant growth. The hypothesis is motivated by the rationale that, as native species' documented specialist tendencies enable them to be uniquely suited to an area's particular ecological niche (Ziska, Blumenthal, Runion, Hunt, & Diaz-Soltero, 2011), climate change's distortion of niche-specific abiotic factors (i.e. temperature and soil moisture levels) will leave the system vulnerable to colonization by generalist invaders. Building on previous principles of native-invasive plant interactions under climate pressures (Walther et al., 2009), this study has implications to advance understanding of the adaptive capacity of Michigan plant ecosystems to climate change impacts, and findings can be used to suggest appropriate mitigative responses to ensure preservation of native species.

Materials and Methods:

A. Study System

This study examined the colonization of Michigan native *Rudbeckia hirta* stands by invasive *Centaurea maculosa* in the presence of simulated climate change effects. Data reveal the impacts of forecasted climate change on the competitive advantages of invasive species in Michigan prairies. Experimentation was conducted at the author's residence with some materials provided by the Matthaei Botanical Gardens.

B. Experimental Design

Plots of native *R. hirta* were planted with increasing densities of invasive *C. maculosa*. Plots were exposed to varying levels of elevated temperature and precipitation disturbance treatments throughout seed germination and plant growth phases. This allowed for the evaluation of invasive species' success in colonization as forecasted climate change impacts become more severe. After a growth period of four weeks, the masses of dehydrated *R. hirta* individuals were recorded using a gram balance. The experiment utilized four replicates for each of 25 unique plot types, for a total of 100 plots (see Fig. 1). Two sets of controls were used. The first measured *R. hirta* growth at all disturbance levels without the addition of *C. maculosa*, allowing baseline native plant growth to be assessed across climate conditions without invasive pressures. The second measured *R.*

hirta growth under all *C. maculosa* density levels without any added climate disturbance, allowing for the isolated assessment of the invasive species on *R. hirta* without climate change. Together, these controls provided a standard of comparison against which the isolated and interactive effects of each independent variable were evaluated.

Each plot was contained in a small plastic holder of dimensions 2.76 x 2.76 x 3.15 inches. Holders were filled 1 inch from the surface with potting soil of similar nutrient composition to that found in Michigan prairies (Kost, Albert, Cohen, Slaughter, Schillo, Weber & Chapman, 2007). Five native *R. hirta* seeds were placed in the center of each plot. The required density of invasive *C. maculosa* seeds was then placed around the target uniformly on all sides (see Fig. 1). A thin layer of soil was applied to cover the seeds. Disturbance treatments simulated combined heat wave and flood events through increasingly intensive watering regimens [10, 20, 30, 40 and 50 milliliters per day] and exposure durations to a heated growing table [0, 1, 2, 3, 4 hours per day]. The table heated soils to approximately 90 degrees F, above the preferred germination temperature for Michigan prairie plants, which is around 75 degrees F.

Environmental Disturbance Level → C. maculosa (Invasive) Density ↓	No Added Disturbance (control)	Low Added Disturbance Treatment	Moderate Added Disturbance Treatment	High Added Disturbance Treatment	Very High Added Disturbance Treatment
0 seeds (control)	4 replicates (*dual control*)	4 replicates (control)	4 replicates (control)	4 replicates (control)	4 replicates (control)
2 seeds	4 replicates (*control*)	4 replicates	4 replicates	4 replicates	4 replicates
4 seeds	4 replicates (*control*)	4 replicates	4 replicates	4 replicates	4 replicates
8 seeds	4 replicates (*control*)	4 replicates	4 replicates	4 replicates	4 replicates
16 seeds	4 replicates (*control*)	4 replicates	4 replicates	4 replicates	4 replicates

Figure 1: *Experimental design featuring increasing levels of climate change and invasive species threats to native R. hirta.*

C. Statistical Analysis

Given that the level of climate disturbance and *C. maculosa* density are both ordinal categorical independent variables, and given that the mass of *R. hirta* is a continuous quantitative dependent variable, the data were suited to analysis by two-part ANOVA to determine if differences in *R. hirta* mass varied at statistically significant levels among treatments. This statistical method allowed for a comparison of the differential in means between *R. hirta* growth under isolated invasive pressure, isolated climate pressure, combined invasive and climate pressures, and in the absence of any experimental treatments. As such, the two-part ANOVA illustrated the degree to which the hypothesized competitive advantages of the invasive *C. maculosa* were statistically manifested in suppressed growth of *R. hirta*, enabling conclusions to be drawn on the propensity for climate change to act in concert with invasive species to accelerate harm to native ecosystems.

Results:

Environ-mental → Distur-bance Level	No Added Disturbance	Low Added Disturbance Treatment	Moderate Added Disturbance Treatment	High Added Disturbance Treatment	Very High Added Disturbance Treatment
C. maculosa (Invasive) Density ↓					
0 seeds (control)	5.0, 5.0, 4.8, 4.9	4.6, 4.7, 4.5, 4.5	4.0, 4.2, 4.0, 4.4	3.0, 3.1, 3.2, 3.1	2.0, 2.3, 2.4, 2.0
2 seeds	4.8, 4.8, 4.8, 4.6	4.5, 4.5, 4,3, 4,0	4.2, 4.3, 3.9, 3,8	3.2, 2.7, 3.0. 2.4	2.0, 1.9, 1.9, 2.0
4 seeds	4.5, 4.4, 4.1, 4.4	4.3, 3.8, 3.6, 4.0	3.6, 3.6, 3.4, 3.1	2.2, 2.3, 2.5, 2.5	1.4, 1.6, 1.6, 1.5
8 seeds	4.0, 4.2, 3.9, 3.9	3.7, 3.8, 3.5, 3.5	3.4. 3.0, 2.9, 3.1	2.4, 2.0, 1.9, 2.1	1.3, 1.3, 1.3, 1.3
16 seeds	3.5, 3.3, 3.2, 3.5	2.9, 2.6, 2.8, 2.7	2.4, 2.1, 2.1, 2.3	1.5, 2.0, 1.5, 1.4	0.7, 0.9, 1.1, 1.2

Figure 2: *Raw data table of dehydrated R. hirta mass (g) when exposed to increasing climate disturbances and invasive pressures by C. maculosa*

Data compiled in Fig. 2 above measure the effect of two categorical independent variables—(1) the level of climate disturbance to which plots were exposed and (2) the density of invasive *C. maculosa* with which native *R. hirta* contended—on the dehydrated biomass of native *R. hirta*. Several key trends are derived:

I. Effect of Climate Disturbance Level on *R. hirta* Biomass:

Observation of the data reveals that as the level of combined heat and flooding stress increased on plant populations, mean native *R. hirta* biomass decreased substantially. At any given density of invasive species, native *R. hirta* performed the best among all climate conditions under the control of no added disturbance, where native samples measured approximately 4.8 grams on average. This indicates that optimal growth conditions for *R. hirta* occurred when climate change impacts were minimized. *R. hirta* grew slightly less well under the low and moderate disturbance treatments as mean mass dropped to approximately 4.0 grams. Additional large negative effects were recorded at high and very high disturbance levels, as *R. hirta* mass dropped to 3.0 and 2.25 grams respectively (see Figure 3 below). Overall, a strong negative correlation between climate disturbance and *R. hirta* biomass was discovered. A two-part analysis of variation (ANOVA) test performed on the data in SPSS revealed that growth of native *R. hirta* individuals was hindered by increasing climate change disturbances at a statistically significant level. The p value of 0.000 is less than 0.05, thus the null hypothesis that there is no significant effect is rejected.

Figure 3:

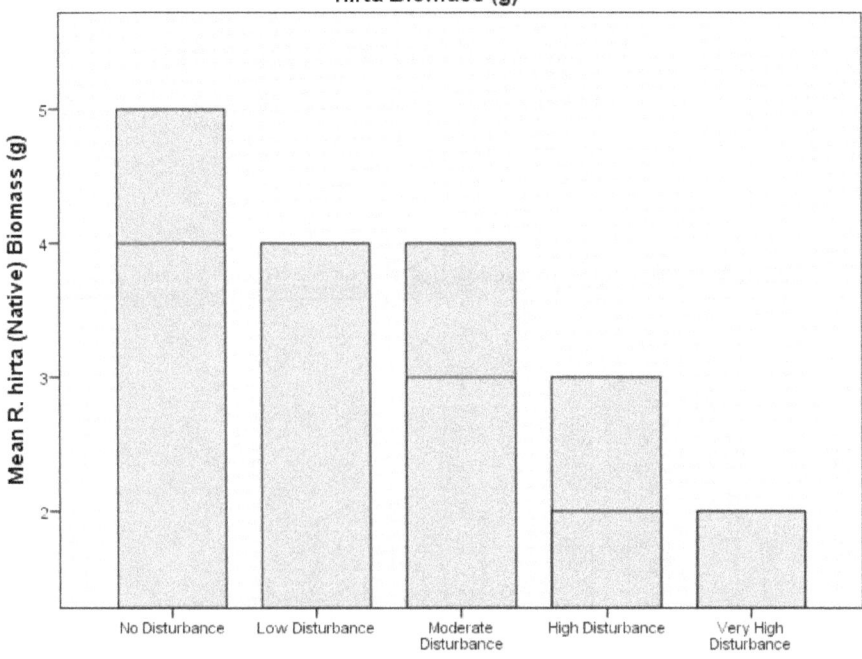

Effect of Increasing Climate Change Change Disturbance Intensity on Mean R. hirta Biomass (g)

II. Effect of Invasive *C. maculosa* Density on *R. hirta* Biomass:

Data indicate that as the density of invasive *C. maculosa* increased in plots co-occupied by native *R. hirta*, mean *R. hirta* biomass decreased substantially. At any given level of climate disturbance, native *R. hirta* performed the best among all invasive *C. maculosa* densities at the control of zero added *C. maculosa* seeds, where native samples measured approximately 4.7 grams. This indicates that optimal native plant growth conditions occurred, as expected, in the absence of any interspecific competition. As *C. maculosa* density increased to 2, 4, and 8 seed levels, corresponding *R. hirta* biomass decreased slightly to approximately 3.6 grams. A large drop in *R. hirta* performance to an average of 2.0 g was recorded as *C. maculosa* density increased to 16 seeds, the highest invasive species treatment. This data trend reveals a strong negative correlation between severity of invasive colonization and level of native biomass growth (see Figure 4 below). A two-part analysis of variation (ANOVA) test performed on the data in SPSS revealed that growth of native *R. hirta* individuals is hindered by *increasing C. maculosa* density at a statistically significant level. The p value of 0.000 is less than 0.05, thus the null hypothesis that there is no significant effect is rejected.

Figure 4:

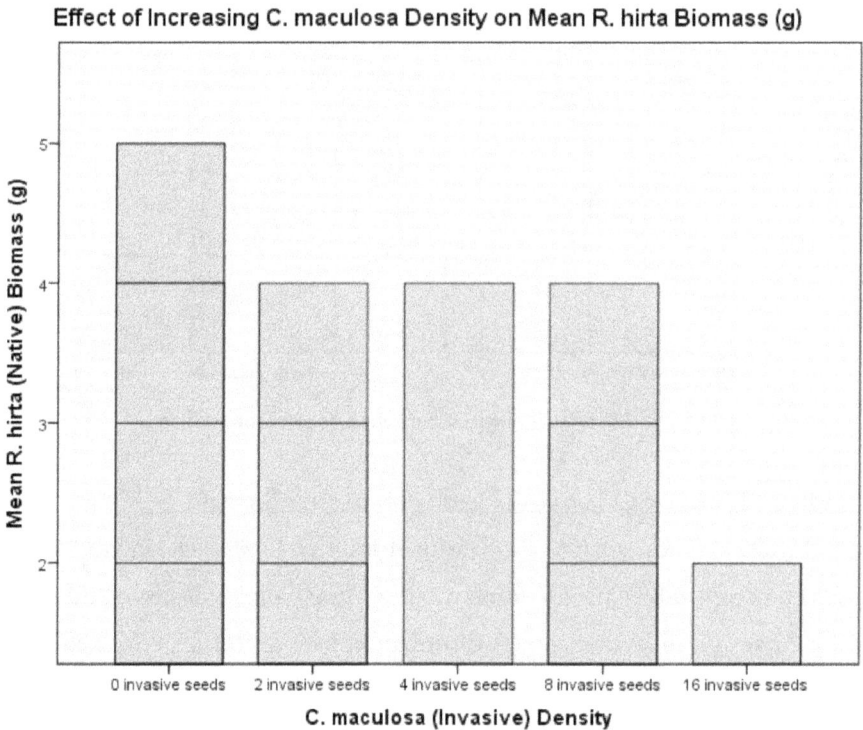

Effect of Increasing C. maculosa Density on Mean R. hirta Biomass (g)

III. Interactive Effect of Climate Disturbance and *C. maculosa* Density on *R. hirta* Biomass:

Data suggest that simultaneous climate change and invasive species treatments have a significant combined negative effect on *R. hirta* biomass. A comparative "bubble map" (see Figure 5 below) was constructed in SPSS to showcase mean *R. hirta* mass under the influence of both treatment types. Wider circles reflecting relatively larger average *R. hirta* masses approaching 5 grams are concentrated in the lower left-hand corner of the figure, where climate and invasive treatments were both low. The smallest circles, illustrating smaller average *R. hirta* masses around 2 grams are clustered in the upper right-hand corner, under high and very high climate disturbance levels and *C. maculosa* densities. A two-part analysis of variation (ANOVA) test performed on the data in SPSS revealed that there is a statistically significant interaction between *C. maculosa* density and climate change disturbances on *R. hirta* growth. The p value of 0.021 is less than 0.05, thus the null hypothesis that there is no significant effect is rejected. These results demonstrate that native plant species face numerous tiers of threats that, when acting in concert, create a multiplier effect accelerating biomass loss in native plant ecosystems.

Figure 5:

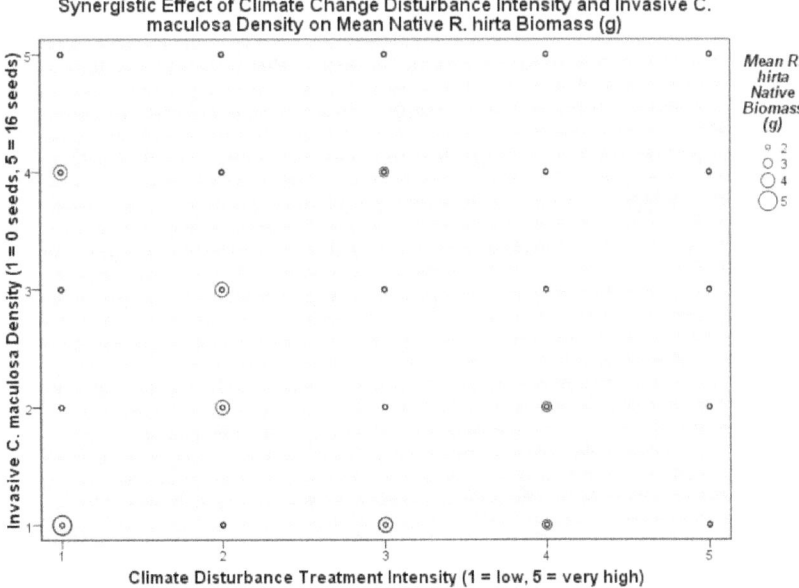

Synergistic Effect of Climate Change Disturbance Intensity and Invasive C. maculosa Density on Mean Native R. hirta Biomass (g)

Discussion and Conclusions:

This study's proposed experimental design is derived from an analogous 2-year study on 63 native and non-native European grasses (Haeuser, Dawson, & van Kleunen, 2017) but relatively few have become invasive. Low climatic suitability may be limiting. 2. Here we tested how colonization ability (a prerequisite for invasion. In that study, absolute colonization success of invasives was found to increase proportionally with climate disturbance. However, researchers base their findings on adverse impacts observed on native grasses, rather than sewn species (such as the Michigan wildflowers examined herein). Additionally, Haeuser et al. introduce heat waves alone, overlooking flooding stresses that figure prominently in forecasted climate change effects, particularly in the Northern Hemisphere. As such, there is a vacancy in the literature which is filled by this study's explicit focus on a wildflower prairie context and introduction of multiple dimensions of disturbance (heat stress *and* flooding).

Data from this experiment illustrating that *R. hirta* mass decreases at higher levels of climate disturbance and at higher concentrations of invasive *C. maculosa* support the proposed hypothesis that forecasted climate change will increase native plant vulnerability to negative impacts from invasive species colonization. Indeed, these trends identify climate change as a key disruptor responsible for increasing deviation from ideal native plant growing conditions on Michigan prairies. Furthermore, the rationale that invasive species' elevated thermo- and moisture tolerance provides a competitive advantage over native species under climate change pressures appears to be substantiated. Findings of a statistically significant interactive effect of disturbance level and invasive density treatments highlights multi-dimensional threats to future native plant success and the urgency with which relevant conservation techniques must be mobilized.

The study faced limitations in both time and scope: only one growing season was examined, thus, no conclusions may be drawn regarding potentially long-term competitive advantages of invasives over multiple seasons. Additionally, by merely testing the influence of one (among many known) invasive plants on

Michigan prairies, this study disregards potential effects of multiple colonizing species across native plant stands, as well as the differential colonization potentials of various invasive plant species under particular climate conditions. Finally, the use of only four replicates for each combination of *C. maculosa* density and disturbance level produced a relatively large degree of variance between individual replicates; more time and resources would allow for larger-scale future experimentation that could increase the sample size and ensure the broader generalizability of the data.

Results from this study outline pressing and severe threats to the native species composition and productivity of Michigan plant ecosystems. As the combustion of fossil fuels and corresponding emission of greenhouse gases continues to accelerate on a global scale, additional research will be critical in diagramming ecological impacts and suggesting mechanisms to combat biodiversity loss and declines in the value of population-sustaining ecosystem services. This study draws particular attention to the propensity of climate change to exacerbate invasive species-induced damage and strengthens a growing—yet incomplete—body of literature cataloguing the numerous adverse dimensions of climate change on terrestrial biosystems.

Acknowledgements:

I would like to thank the Matthaei Botanical Gardens for providing equipment necessary for the completion of this study; Abagail Potts and Professor Lynn Carpenter for their tireless editing of drafts and invaluable feedback on research design considerations; Lorena Cortes-Torres for ordering materials and coordinating logistics; Maggie Mianecke for collecting and sharing *C. maculosa* seeds; Peter Arvan and Amy Chang for tolerating the month-long occupation of their basement with plants.

Literature Cited:

Diez, J. M., D'Antonio, C. M., Dukes, J. S., Grosholz, E. D., Olden, J. D., Sorte, C. J. B., ... Miller, L. P. (2012). Will extreme climatic events facilitate biological invasions? *Frontiers in Ecology and the Environment.* https://doi.org/10.1890/110137

Dukes, J. S., Pontius, J., Orwig, D., Garnas, J. R., Rodgers, V. L., Brazee, N., ... Ayres, M. (2009). Responses of insect pests, pathogens, and invasive plant species to climate change in the forests of northeastern North America: What can we predict? This article is one of a selection of papers from NE Forests 2100: A Synthesis of Climate Change Impacts o. *Canadian Journal of Forest Research, 39*(2), 231–248. https://doi.org/10.1139/X08-171

French, K., Robinson, S. A., & Lia, J. (2017). Thermotolerance capacities of native and exotic coastal plants will lead to changes in species composition under increased heat waves. *Conservation Physiology, 5*(1985), 1–10. https://doi.org/10.1093/conphys/cox029

Haeuser, E., Dawson, W., & van Kleunen, M. (2017). The effects of climate warming and disturbance on the colonization potential of ornamental alien plant species. *Journal of Ecology, 105*(6), 1698–1708. https://doi.org/10.1111/1365-2745.12798

Hayhoe, K., J. VanDorn, T. Croley, II, N. Schlegal, and D. Wuebbles, 2010: Regional climate change projections for Chicago and the US Great Lakes. Journal of Great Lakes Research, 36, 7-21, doi:10.1016/j.jglr.2010.03.012

Hellmann, J. J., Byers, J. E., Bierwagen, B. G., & Dukes, J. S. (2008). Five Potential Consequences of Climate Change for Invasive Species. *Conservation Biology, 22*(3), 534–543. https://doi.org/10.1111/j.1523-1739.2008.00951.

Kost, M.A., D.A. Albert, J.G. Cohen, B.S. Slaughter, R.K. Schillo, C.R.Weber, and K.A. Chapman. 2007. Natural Communities of Michigan: Classification and Description. Michigan Natural Features Inventory, Report Number 2007-21, Lansing, MI. pp. 1-314.

Thuiller, W., Albert, C., Araújo, M. B., Berry, P. M., Cabeza, M., Guisan, A., … Zimmermann, N. E. (2008). Predicting global change impacts on plant species' distributions: Future challenges. *Perspectives in Plant Ecology, Evolution and Systematics, 9*(3–4), 137–152. https://doi.org/10.1016/j.ppees.2007.09.004

Walther, G., Roques, A., Hulme, P. E., Sykes, M. T., Ku, I., & Zobel, M. (2009). Alien species in a warmer world: risks and opportunities. *Trends in Ecology & Evolution, 24*(12), 686–693. Retrieved from http://space.skyrocket.de/doc_sdat/tiungsat-1.htm

Zerebecki, R. A., & Sorte, C. J. B. (2011). Temperature tolerance and stress proteins as mechanisms of invasive species success. *PLoS ONE, 6*(4). https://doi.org/10.1371/journal.pone.0014806

Ziska, L. H., Blumenthal, D. M., Runion, G. B., Hunt, E. R., & Diaz-Soltero, H. (2011). Invasive species and climate change: An agronomic perspective. *Climatic Change, 105*(1), 13–42. https://doi.org/10.1007/s10584-010-9879-5

Appendix of Data Analysis, Graphs, and SPSS Code

Step 1: Cleaning/Preparing the Data for Analysis

- Data was assessed in SPSS Statistical Analysis Software (IBM), an R alternative
- Key for data labels
  - Climate Disturbance Level (Independent Variable 1)
    - No disturbance: input as "1"
    - Low disturbance: input as "2"
    - Moderate disturbance: input as "3"
    - High disturbance: input as "4"
    - Very high disturbance: input as "5"

  - *C. maculosa* (Invasive) Density (Independent Variable 2)
    - 0 seeds: input as "1"
    - 2 seeds: input as "2"
    - 4 seeds: input as "3"
    - 8 seeds: input as "4"
    - 16 seeds: input as "5"

Climate Disturbance Level Indep. 1	C. maculosa Density Indep. 2	R. hirta Mass (g) Dep.
1	1	5
1	1	5
1	1	4.8
1	1	4.9
1	2	4.8
1	2	4.8
1	2	4.8
1	2	4.6
1	3	4.5

1	3	4.4
1	3	4.1
1	3	4.4
1	4	4
1	4	4.2
1	4	3.9
1	4	3.9
1	5	3.5
1	5	3.3
1	5	3.2
1	5	3.5
2	1	4.6
2	1	4.7
2	1	4.5
2	1	4.5
2	2	4.5
2	2	4.5
2	2	4.3
2	2	4
2	3	4.3
2	3	3.8
2	3	3.6
2	3	4
2	4	3.7
2	4	3.8
2	4	3.5
2	4	3.5
2	5	2.9
2	5	2.6
2	5	2.8
2	5	2.7
3	1	4
3	1	4.2

3	1	4
3	1	4.4
3	2	4.2
3	2	4.3
3	2	3.9
3	2	3.8
3	3	3.6
3	3	3.6
3	3	3.4
3	3	3.1
3	4	3.4
3	4	3
3	4	2.9
3	4	3.1
3	5	2.4
3	5	2.1
3	5	2.1
3	5	2.3
4	1	3
4	1	3.1
4	1	3.2
4	1	3.1
4	2	3.2
4	2	2.7
4	2	3
4	2	2.4
4	3	2.2
4	3	2.3
4	3	2.5
4	3	2.5
4	4	2.4
4	4	2
4	4	1.9

4	4	2.1
4	5	1.5
4	5	2
4	5	1.5
4	5	1.4
5	1	2
5	1	2.3
5	1	2.4
5	1	2
5	2	2
5	2	1.9
5	2	1.9
5	2	2
5	3	1.4
5	3	1.6
5	3	1.6
5	3	1.5
5	4	1.3
5	4	1.3
5	4	1.3
5	4	1.3
5	5	0.7
5	5	0.9
5	5	1.1
5	5	1.2

Step 2: ANOVA conducted in SPSS

```
UNIANOVA NativeMassGrams BY DisturbanceLevel InvasiveDensity
  /METHOD=SSTYPE(3)
  /INTERCEPT=INCLUDE
  /EMMEANS=TABLES(DisturbanceLevel)
  /EMMEANS=TABLES(InvasiveDensity)
  /EMMEANS=TABLES(DisturbanceLevel*InvasiveDensity)
  /CRITERIA=ALPHA(.05)
  /DESIGN=DisturbanceLevel InvasiveDensity
DisturbanceLevel*InvasiveDensity.
```

Univariate Analysis of Variance

Between-Subjects Factors

		N
DisturbanceLevel	1	20
	2	20
	3	20
	4	20
	5	20
InvasiveDensity	1	20
	2	20
	3	20
	4	20
	5	20

Tests of Between-Subjects Effects

Dependent Variable: NativeMassGrams

Source	Type III Sum of Squares	df	Mean Square	F	Sig. (p)
Corrected Model	129.592[a]	24	5.400	153.545	.000
Intercept	960.380	1	960.380	27309.387	.000
DisturbanceLevel	96.186	4	24.047	683.790	.000
InvasiveDensity	32.257	4	8.064	229.318	.000
DisturbanceLevel * InvasiveDensity	1.149	16	.072	2.041	.021
Error	2.638	75	.035		
Total	1092.610	100			
Corrected Total	132.230	99			

a. R Squared = .980 (Adjusted R Squared = .974)

Estimated Marginal Means

1. Disturbance Level

Dependent Variable: NativeMassGrams

DisturbanceLevel	Mean	Std. Error	95% Confidence Interval	
			Lower Bound	Upper Bound
1	4.280	.042	4.196	4.364
2	3.840	.042	3.756	3.924
3	3.390	.042	3.306	3.474
4	2.400	.042	2.316	2.484
5	1.585	.042	1.501	1.669

2. InvasiveDensity

Dependent Variable: NativeMassGrams

InvasiveDensity	Mean	Std. Error	95% Confidence Interval	
			Lower Bound	Upper Bound
1	3.785	.042	3.701	3.869
2	3.580	.042	3.496	3.664
3	3.120	.042	3.036	3.204
4	2.825	.042	2.741	2.909
5	2.185	.042	2.101	2.269

3. DisturbanceLevel * InvasiveDensity

Dependent Variable: NativeMassGrams

DisturbanceLevel	InvasiveDensity	Mean	Std. Error	95% Confidence Interval	
				Lower Bound	Upper Bound
1	1	4.925	.094	4.738	5.112
	2	4.750	.094	4.563	4.937
	3	4.350	.094	4.163	4.537
	4	4.000	.094	3.813	4.187
	5	3.375	.094	3.188	3.562

2	1	4.575	.094	4.388	4.762
	2	4.325	.094	4.138	4.512
	3	3.925	.094	3.738	4.112
	4	3.625	.094	3.438	3.812
	5	2.750	.094	2.563	2.937
3	1	4.150	.094	3.963	4.337
	2	4.050	.094	3.863	4.237
	3	3.425	.094	3.238	3.612
	4	3.100	.094	2.913	3.287
	5	2.225	.094	2.038	2.412
4	1	3.100	.094	2.913	3.287
	2	2.825	.094	2.638	3.012
	3	2.375	.094	2.188	2.562
	4	2.100	.094	1.913	2.287
	5	1.600	.094	1.413	1.787
5	1	2.175	.094	1.988	2.362
	2	1.950	.094	1.763	2.137
	3	1.525	.094	1.338	1.712
	4	1.300	.094	1.113	1.487
	5	.975	.094	.788	1.162

Graph 1:

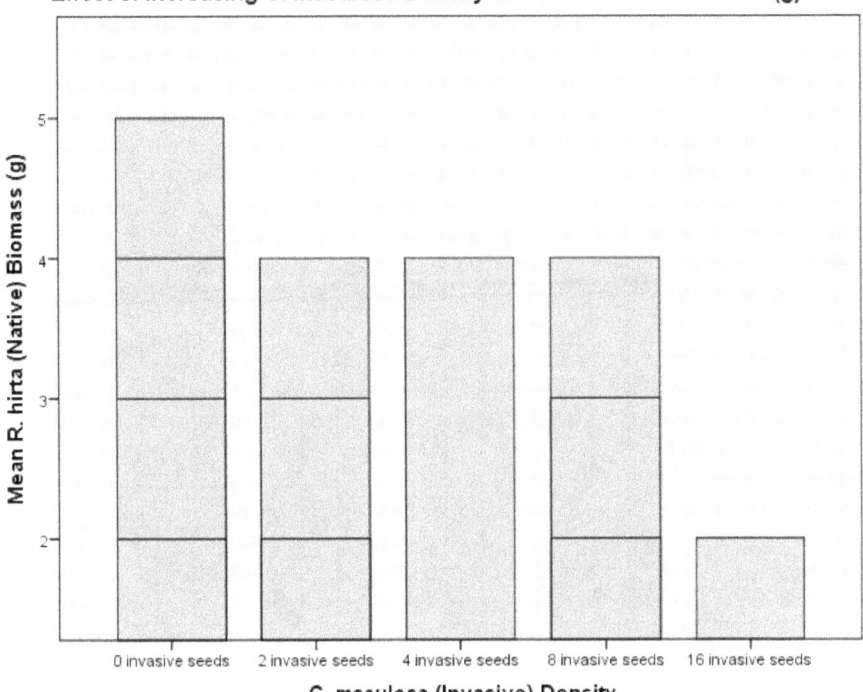

* Chart Builder.

```
GGRAPH
  /GRAPHDATASET NAME="graphdataset" VARIABLES=InvasiveDensity
NativeMassGrams MISSING=LISTWISE
    REPORTMISSING=NO
  /GRAPHSPEC SOURCE=INLINE.
BEGIN GPL
  SOURCE: s=userSource(id("graphdataset"))
  DATA: InvasiveDensity=col(source(s), name("InvasiveDensity"),
unit.category())
  DATA: NativeMassGrams=col(source(s), name("NativeMassGrams"),
unit.category())
  GUIDE: axis(dim(1), label("InvasiveDensity"))
  GUIDE: axis(dim(2), label("NativeMassGrams"))
  ELEMENT: interval(position(InvasiveDensity*NativeMassGrams),
shape.interior(shape.square))
END GPL.
```

Graph 2:

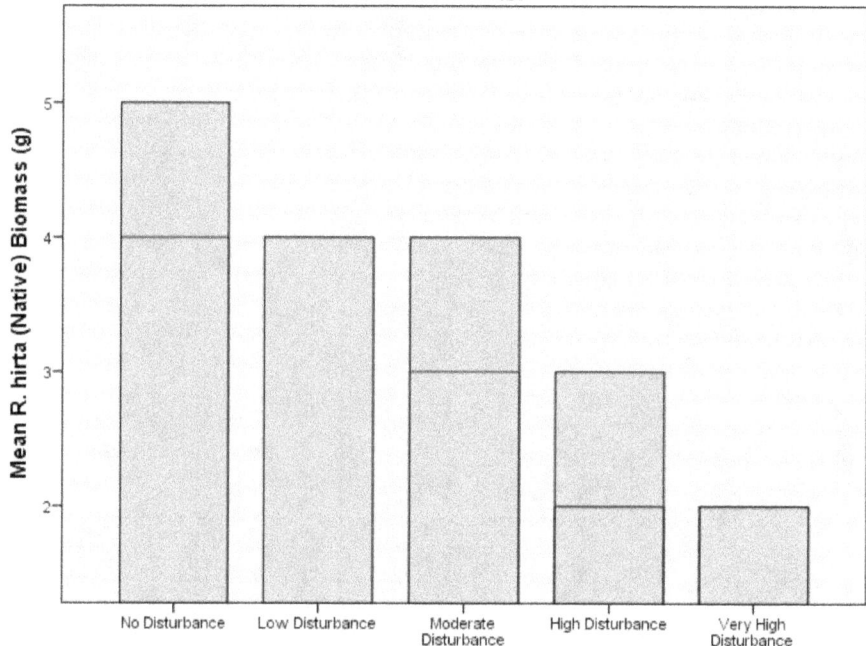

Effect of Increasing Climate Change Change Disturbance Intensity on Mean R. hirta Biomass (g)

```
* Chart Builder.
GGRAPH
  /GRAPHDATASET NAME="graphdataset" VARIABLES=DisturbanceLevel
NativeMassGrams MISSING=LISTWISE
    REPORTMISSING=NO
  /GRAPHSPEC SOURCE=INLINE.
BEGIN GPL
  SOURCE: s=userSource(id("graphdataset"))
  DATA: DisturbanceLevel=col(source(s),
name("DisturbanceLevel"), unit.category())
  DATA: NativeMassGrams=col(source(s), name("NativeMassGrams"),
unit.category())
  GUIDE: axis(dim(1), label("DisturbanceLevel"))
  GUIDE: axis(dim(2), label("NativeMassGrams"))
  ELEMENT: interval(position(DisturbanceLevel*NativeMassGrams),
shape.interior(shape.square))
END GPL.
```

Graph 3:

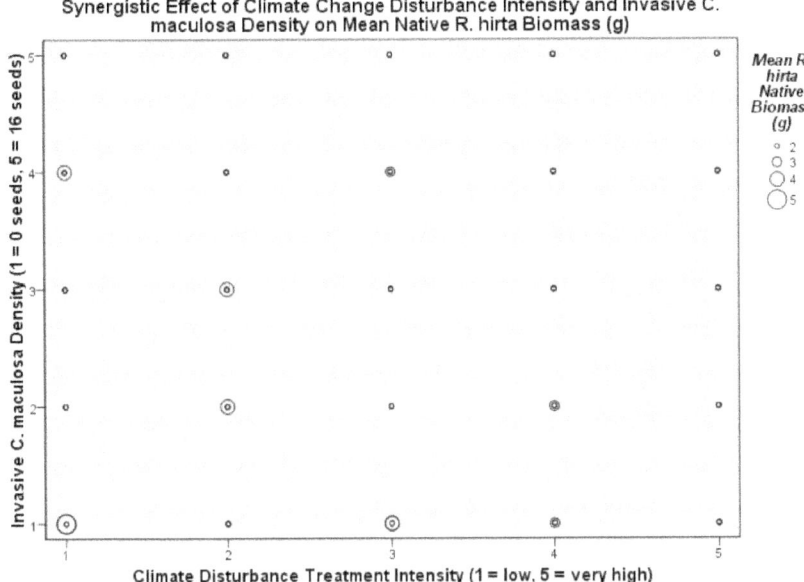

```
GGRAPH
  /GRAPHDATASET NAME="graphdataset"
    VARIABLES=InvasiveDensity[LEVEL=nominal]
NativeMassGrams[LEVEL=nominal]
    DisturbanceLevel[LEVEL=nominal]
    MISSING=LISTWISE REPORTMISSING=NO
  /GRAPHSPEC SOURCE=VIZTEMPLATE(NAME="Bubble Plot"
[LOCATION=LOCAL]
    MAPPING( "sizes"="NativeMassGrams"[DATASET="graphdataset"]
    "x"="DisturbanceLevel"[DATASET="graphdataset"]
"y"="InvasiveDensity"[DATASET="graphdataset"]
    "Title"='Synergistic Effect of Climate Change Disturbance
Intensity and Invasive C. maculosa '+
    'Density on Mean Native R. hirta Biomass (g)'))
    VIZSTYLESHEET="Traditional"[LOCATION=LOCAL]
    LABEL='BUBBLE PLOT: NativeMassGrams-DisturbanceLevel-
InvasiveDensity'
    DEFAULTTEMPLATE=NO.
```

Excellence in Upper-Level Writing (Sciences)

Current research on exoplanets and the search for habitable worlds
by Elizabeth Stanley
From Writing 400: Writing and Research in the Sciences
Nominated by Jimmy Brancho

Elizabeth's essay offers an accessible and methodically educational look into detecting and characterizing exoplanets. I was impressed by the review's structure, which first armed the reader with a basic rundown of physical measurements and concepts before demonstrating how they were applied to the now-famous TRAPPIST-1 system. Elizabeth's paper excels in its potential to teach a novice reader how these measurements are effective. Thoughtfully researched and written with an awareness of the intended audience, I think this is a very strong upper-level sample.

Jimmy Brancho

Current research on exoplanets and the search for habitable worlds

0. Abstract

In the past two decades years, the field of astrobiology has developed from a mere concept to a flourishing academic field. Over 3500 exoplanets have already been confirmed and discovered over a relatively short period of time and increasing sophistication of technology has allowed researchers to characterize individual exoplanets and even evaluate their potential habitability. One of the core goals of the astrobiological field is to discover whether life could be supported on planets besides Earth, which focuses and shapes the discussion surrounding exoplanets. This review includes an overview and description of the past and current methodologies which are used to discover exoplanets. Methods of determining an exoplanet's potential habitability are also given. Finally, a case study of the planets in the TRAPPIST-1 M dwarf star system is provided as a real-world example of how the potential habitability of exoplanets can be evaluated, and how research may proceed in the future with the advent of new and improved technology.

1. Introduction

The existence of planets and civilizations other than our own is an idea that has fascinated humanity for centuries, from the concepts of other worlds described in ancient literature to modern science fiction in the early 19th century. Messages such as the 1974 Arecibo message[1] and spacecraft like the 1977 Voyager 1 and 2[2] were sent into interstellar space containing information on Earth and its inhabitants, intended for any extraterrestrial life that encountered it. However, extraterrestrial worlds or exoplanets[3] only shifted from being merely a fiction to a scientific reality when the first exoplanets were discovered around a pulsar in 1992 by radio astronomers Wolszczan & Frail. As technology advanced and more planets were discovered, the search for exoplanets became an increasingly prominent area of astronomical research. Multiple ground- and space-based telescopes have been dedicated to the search for exoplanets, including current missions such as the Kepler/K2 and HARPS missions, as well as future missions such as the JWST and CHEOPS. Currently, over 3500 exoplanets have been found[4], with more constantly being confirmed or discovered.

The number of exoplanets that we can detect and characterize has led to the development of a new area of study: astrobiology. Astrobiology is a multidisciplinary field combining space, earth, and biological sciences with a focus on searching for the answer to three questions: how does life begin and evolve, does life exist elsewhere in the universe, and what is the future of life on Earth and beyond (Des Marais et al. 2008). Studying exoplanets in detail allows us to calculate certain properties that can be used to determine physical characteristics of the planet to the point we can begin to evaluate its potential habitability. A habitable planet is generally characterized as a planet that can maintain liquid water on a geological timescale, as liquid water is necessary to all living organisms we are aware of (Kasting et al. 1993). Habitable exoplanets generally lie in

---

1   https://www.seti.org/seti-institute/project/details/arecibo-message
2   https://voyager.jpl.nasa.gov/
3   An exoplanet is defined as a planet which orbits a star outside the solar system. Oxford Dictionary of English, 3rd edition. http://www.oxfordreference.com/
4   https://exoplanetarchive.ipac.caltech.edu/ as of 10/04/2018

the habitable zone, the area around a star where the surface temperature of a planet there would allow liquid water to exist, although other factors such as the exoplanet's atmospheric makeup also have an impact on the surface temperature. While the technology that can characterize exoplanetary environments is still in its early stages, as more precise recording instrumentation is developed we will be able to better understand exoplanets and evaluate their habitability. In the future, instead of sending spacecraft and messages out into the void, we can direct them towards systems that we have calculated to have more potential to be habitable, in hopes that we can confirm extraterrestrial life exists.

This review aims to give an overview of the search for extraterrestrial planets up to the present day with a focus on potential habitability. It will describe the main methods of detection that have been used by past and current missions to locate exoplanets, as well as discuss future missions and the specific data they hope to collect [Section 2]. We then provide an overview of what factors determine a planet's potential habitability and how some of these factors may be associated with the existence of extraterrestrial life [Section 3]. As an example of how a system might be evaluated for habitability can be found in the case study of TRAPPIST-1, a recently discovered system which contains 7 planets orbiting an M dwarf star [Section 4.] A brief look at the potential future work in this field will conclude the review [Section 5].

2. Methods of Detection

The first exoplanets orbiting a star were discovered in 1992 around the millisecond pulsar PSR 1257+12. Pulsars are rapidly rotating neutron stars whose rotation produces regularly 'pulsing' radio emissions. As a result, irregularities in the period of the radio pulses can be used to calculate the movement of the pulsar. Anomalies observed in the pulsation period of PSR 1257+12 of $\pm$ 0.7 ms^{-1} were greater than the standard variation in pulsars of that type, which warranted further investigation by its researchers. They concluded that the movements of the star causing these anomalies were most likely due to the gravitational effects of two planets orbiting the pulsar with orbital periods of 98.2 and 66.6 days (Wolszczan & Frail 1992).

Since then, technology has developed significantly, so we can detect more exoplanets with higher degrees of accuracy. Still, it is a challenge to build telescopes with a high enough resolution to visually image exoplanets/resolve them from their star, so very few exoplanets have been observed in this way. Instead, methods of indirect observation are more often used to detect exoplanets. Figure 1 (following page) displays some of the most common methods of exoplanet detection.

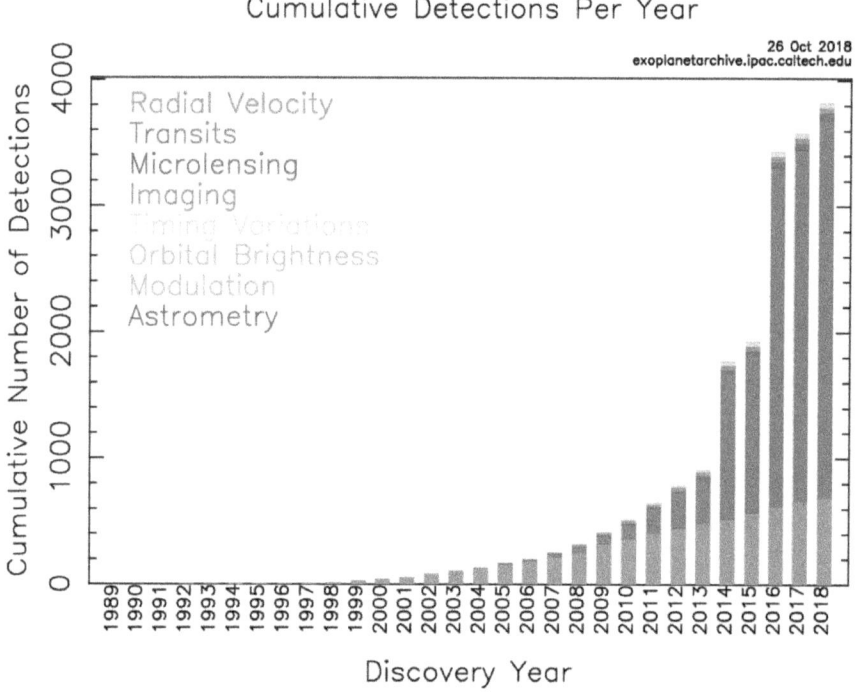

Figure 1 – the total number of detected exoplanets per year by detection method. Until 2014, the radial velocity method (red) had found the most planets. The Kepler mission was launched in 2009 and its K2 phase began in late 2013, significantly increasing the number of transit (green) planets discovered. Every method besides imaging (blue) are methods of indirect observation. Figure reproduced from https://exoplanetarchive.ipac.caltech.edu/.

2.1 Radial Velocity

The radial velocity method of detecting planets is one of the oldest ways of exoplanetary detection. Until 2013, the majority of exoplanets had been found with radial velocity detection, and today the method is still used in exoplanet search projects such as the European Southern Observatory's High Accuracy Radial velocity Planet Searcher (HARPS) spectrograph[5].

The radial velocity method relies on Doppler shift, a phenomena where an object's movement towards or away from the observer causes its emission wavelengths to be compressed (movement towards, increases frequency) or stretched (movement away, lowers frequency). This kind of shift can be caused by an orbiting planet. The relationship between the mass and velocity of two orbiting bodies, a star and a planet, is given below:

$$\mathbf{M_p V_p = M_s V_s}$$

The velocity of the star (V_s) is proportional to the mass of the planet (M_p) over the mass of the star (M_s) (Wright 2017). The star is always more massive than the planet, but if the mass of the planet is closer to the mass of the planet, the V_s induced will be proportionally greater, resulting in a more noticeable Doppler shift. Additionally, if the planet is closer to the star, the gravitational force it exerts on the star will be greater and also increase the Doppler shift (Fischer et al. 2014). Therefore, the radial velocity method is more suited to discovering exoplanets that are large (relative to the star) and close to the star.

2.2. Transit

The transit method of detection began to be used in the early 20th century shortly after exoplanets began to be discovered with radial velocity calculations. The Convection, Rotation and planetary Transits (CoRoT) telescope launched in 2006 was the first space mission with instrumentation designed to observe planetary transits, and was succeeded by the Kepler/K2 missions which ran for

---

5   https://www.eso.org/sci/facilities/lasilla/instruments/harps.html

over 9 years and discovered over 2600 exoplanets[6].

The transit method involves observing the brightness of a star over an extended time period and analyzing changes in the star's light curve. When an object passes between the star and the observer, the object blocks some of the incident light, causing a dip in the light curve (Fischer et al. 2014) However, variations in brightness can also be caused by stellar activity like sunspots or flares, so observing the star for a longer time period is necessary to confirm that dips in the light curve are caused by an orbiting object and not stellar artefacts. Usually at least three observed transits are required before an exoplanet can be confirmed with the transit method. Where possible, confirmation is also sought by observing the target star with the radial velocity method to estimate the mass of the transiting object to ensure it is a planet and not a smaller, transiting star (Deeg & Alonso 2018).

2.3 Other Methods

As shown in Figure 1, the number of planets detected by the radial velocity and transit methods is significantly larger than the number of planets detected by alternate means. However, other methods do exist for detecting potential exoplanets, including gravitational lensing/microlensing, astrometry, and imaging. These methods detect fewer exoplanets than the radial velocity or transit methods largely because the conditions under which exoplanets can be detected by these methods are more specific than those required for radial velocity or transit detections. Nevertheless, these methods are important to consider as they are capable of detecting planets whose orbits do not fall between the star and the observer, making them undetectable by the radial velocity or transit methods.

Gravitational lensing/microlensing occurs when light from a background star is bent by a star in front of it so that an image of the background star is visible despite it being obscured behind the lensing star. Microlensing is when the lensing star has a planet in orbit around it that also bends light from the background star.

---

6   https://www.nasa.gov/mission_pages/kepler/main/index.html

This method tends towards finding planets that orbit further from their host stars and do not transit in front of them, as this allows the additional lensing caused by the planet to be more distinct from the star lensing. Lensing observations can be done by both ground-based (OGLE) and space-based (Spitzer) telescopes.

Astrometry is similar to the radial velocity method of detection in that it measures the movement of a star due to an orbiting body. Instead of measuring Doppler shift as the star moves perpendicular to the plane of the sky, astrometry involves observing the changes in the star's position in the plane of the sky. This method tends to detect more massive planets that have a larger influence on the star's movement but do not transit in front of the star. Astrometry can also be performed with ground-based telescopes like the Keck telescope as well as space-based telescopes like Gaia, the successor to the Kepler mission.

Imaging is the only method of detection that directly observes the planet; the other aforementioned methods of detection merely infer the planet's existence through observing effects on the star. Directly imaging planets is, however, difficult as planets are significantly smaller and much less luminous than their host stars. A planet needs to be far enough away from the star that it is not overwhelmed by the light from the star and can be distinguished as its own entity. Therefore the direct imaging method is suited to finding planets with orbits further than 5 AU[7] from the star (Fischer et al. 2014). Space-based telescopes are much better for direct imaging than ground-based telescopes, as they do not detect interference created by the Earth's atmosphere. The James Webb Space Telescope set to launch in 2021 will have a lens over two times larger than the lens of the current Hubble Space Telescope, allowing for higher resolution data to be taken and increasing the potential for detecting planets with direct imaging.

3. Habitability and Extraterrestrial Life

After discovering a candidate exoplanet, further investigation can then be undertaken to better determine whether it is capable of supporting life. Life, as

---

7   1 AU = 1.5×10^8 km

we understand it, requires access to liquid water. Some carbon-based life forms, such as tardigrades, can survive for a time without water, but access to liquid water is ultimately necessary for life forms to metabolize and reproduce (Güdel et al. 2014; Des Marais et al. 2008). While the potential for non-carbon (such as silicone) based life forms and alternate solvents to water (such as methane) have not been discounted, the search for habitable exoplanets focuses mainly on those that could support liquid water, since we are certain that life dependent on water exists. A habitable planet also needs to have a solid or liquid surface in order to maintain the stable pressure-temperature conditions needed for life to evolve (Güdel et al. 2014). Gas giant planets, such as Jupiter, therefore do not meet this condition and are ruled out as exoplanets that could be habitable.

3.1 Habitable zone

The habitable zone, or "Goldilocks zone" is the area around a star within which conditions are "just right" to potentially support life. More specifically, it is the distance around a star at which an orbiting planet could maintain the presence of liquid water, as that is one of the necessary elements for supporting life as we know it (Kasting et al. 1993). The location of the habitable zone depends on the temperature (energy output) of the star, as planets must maintain a certain temperature in order to have liquid water. Large stars are hotter and output more energy, and therefore the habitable zones would need to lie further from the star for water to stay as a liquid and not vaporize. Conversely, the habitable zones of smaller, cooler stars are closer to the star so a planet there receives enough incident energy for water there to remain unfrozen.

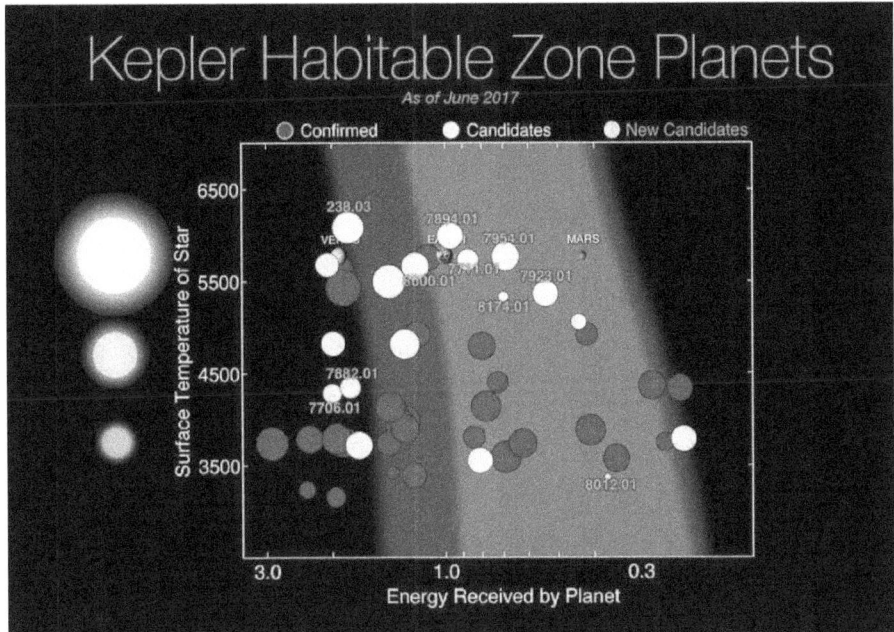

Figure 2 - the conservative (light green) and optimistic (dark green) estimates for the habitable zone calculated for stars of different temperatures. Venus, Earth, and Mars are shown at 6000K (the temperature of our Sun) along with several exoplanets discovered by Kepler. Reproduced from NASA (https://www.nasa.gov/image-feature/ames/kepler/kepler-habitable-zone-planets)

It is important to note that the habitable zone is not a concrete determinant of whether a planet can have liquid water on it, as the atmosphere of the planet can impact its surface temperature. A planet with an atmosphere can retain heat better than a planet with no atmosphere, meaning that planets with thick atmospheres could still have liquid water on their surface despite being outside the base habitable zone of their star. For example, in our Solar System, Earth and Mars both lie within in the conservative boundaries of the habitable zone (Figure 2). While there may be evidence for liquid water having existed on Mars in the past, Mars does not currently have any liquid water present despite being in the habitable zone like Earth. One factor in the difference between Mars and Earth is in the respective atmospheres of the planets. Mars has a very thin atmosphere that is incapable of retaining heat as well as Earth's greenhouse-gas rich atmosphere, which accounts for Mars' lower temperature and lack of surface water. The habitable zone calculation remains a solid metric with which we can search for potentially habitable exoplanets, but as we become able to analyze individual atmospheres of exoplanets our focus can be further narrowed on a case by case basis.

3.2 Emissions

Life forms can cause changes in a planet's atmosphere that can be used as an indicator for their existence. For example, the presence of free oxygen in an atmosphere may be indicative of photosynthesis, a process performed by living organisms. This is evident in Earth's own history in the Great Oxygenation Event, which took place over 3 billion years ago. Cyanobacteria in the oceans photosynthesized and created free oxygen as a byproduct, which built up and eventually became detectable in the Earth's atmosphere (Shields et al. 2016). Therefore, exoplanetary atmospheres with significant oxygenation could be indicative of a similar photosynthetic process taking place.

Human civilization has also caused multiple changes to the biochemical cycles that govern the planet, for example, increased CO_2 emissions due to industrialization and globalization. It is possible that, should intelligent extraterrestrial life exist, their societies also output similar detectable effects, or biosignatures, that we could identify upon observation of an exoplanet's atmosphere.

3.3 Intelligent life

In 1961, a Dr. Frank Drake proposed a formula at a search for extraterrestrial intelligence (SETI) conference to guide the discussion for estimating the probability of extraterrestrial civilizations existing within our galaxy. His formula is duplicated below[8].

$$N = R_* \cdot f_p \cdot n_e \cdot f_l \cdot f_i \cdot f_c \cdot L$$

---

8   Information from https://www.seti.org/drake-equation-index

N = The number of civilizations in the Milky Way Galaxy whose electromagnetic emissions are detectable (ie. civilizations with which human communication is possible)

R^* = The rate of formation of stars suitable for the development of intelligent life.

f_p = The fraction of those stars with planetary systems.

n_e = The number of planets, per solar system, with an environment suitable for life.

f_l = The fraction of suitable planets on which life actually appears.

f_i = The fraction of life bearing planets on which intelligent life emerges.

f_c = The fraction of civilizations that develop a technology that releases detectable signs of their existence into space.

L = The length of time such civilizations release detectable signals into space.

While some of the variables, such as R^*, Fp, and Ne are calculable, or at least can be estimated using current data, the rest of the variables are open to interpretation and depend on the optimism of the person performing the calculation. The equation is intended more as a guiding question to encourage researchers in SETI to consider each variable as they continue to search for extraterrestrial life, and led to considerations such as biosignatures caused by civilization in SETI as detailed above.

4. Case study: the M dwarf system TRAPPIST-1

The TRAnsiting Planets and PlanetesImals Small Telescope (TRAPPIST) observed the M dwarf star TRAPPIST-1 (2MASS J23062928 – 0502285) for 245 hours in 2015 (Gillon et al. 2016). Initial analysis of the data revealed variations in the light curve of the star that could have been caused by transiting bodies. Further observation of TRAPPIST-1 with telescopes including the Very Large Telescope and the Spitzer Space Telescope allowed researchers to attribute these transit-like signatures to the existence of exoplanets.

By 2017, the number of exoplanets confirmed to orbit TRAPPIST-1 had risen from the initial 3 to 7 (Gillon et al. 2017). Three of those planets, TRAPPIST-1e, 1f, and 1g, orbit within the habitable zone of TRAPPIST-1 based on traditional habitable zone calculations (Kasting et al. 1993). However, more of the planets may be habitable if more optimistic metrics for judging a planet's habitability are used (Armstrong et al. 2014; Kopparapu et al. 2013). TRAPPIST-1 is an M dwarf star system, unlike our Solar System, giving rise to different system characteristics that could prove conducive or detrimental to the evolution of life.

4.1 Potential habitability in the TRAPPIST-1 system

M dwarf stars like TRAPPIST-1 are the most numerous types of star in our galaxy. This makes them important candidates in the search for extraterrestrial life for several reasons. First, the number of M dwarf stars that exist increases the probability that a) we will be able to detect exoplanets around one that is b) close enough to us to allow more detailed observation. The TRAPPIST-1 system is relatively close to the Earth at only 12.1 parsecs[9] away, so more detailed observations about its properties can be taken than a star system hundreds of parsecs from us (Gillon et al. 2016).

Small stars like M dwarfs also have a longer main-sequence lifespan than larger stars, providing an appropriate timescale during which life could develop. The evolution of life on Earth is estimated to have taken 3×10^9 to 4×10^9 years, and the estimated main sequence lifespan of our Sun is 10×10^9 years. For comparison, the age of the universe is 13.8×10^{19} years. No M dwarf stars have been observed to have left the main sequence yet, meaning their maximum main sequence age is significantly longer than that of a Sun-like star. This means there is a longer time frame in which life could develop around M dwarf stars.

The small size of M dwarf stars also increases the chances that any planets

---

9   Value from Gillon et al. 2016. 12.1 parsecs = 40 light years = 3.7×10^{14} km. The closest star to Earth is Proxima Centauri, which is 1.3 parsecs or 4.2 light years away.

in orbit around them can be detected, as the ratio between the star and planet size is lower. The lower mass ratio increases the magnitude of the Doppler shift in the star's spectra and therefore its potential for detection with RV. Similarly, the size ratios of the M dwarf and a planet are lower, making any transits more easily detectable as a larger percentage of the star would be covered by the transiting planet. The gravitational force exerted by M dwarfs is low due to their low mass, so objects in orbit around it tend to orbit much closer to the star which increases the chance that a planet will transit in front of the star and thus be detectable.

4.2 Potential issues with habitability in the TRAPPIST-1 system

M dwarf systems were initially dismissed as candidates for habitable exoplanets, but more recent research has reidentified them as viable locations to search (Shields et al. 2016). M dwarfs are active stars and typically exhibit photometric variation characteristic of sunspots or flares, which are caused by radiation and magnetic field activity (Roettenbacher & Kane 2017). As the habitable zone of a small star lies close to the star, any planets in the habitable zone would likely be affected by the stellar activity. However, closer research on the potential habitability of planets around M dwarf stars has suggested that under certain atmospheric conditions, at least some parts of the planet may be able to support liquid water despite the high energy environment (Shields et al. 2016).

The proximity of the habitable zone to the star brings up another potential problem. Planets that orbit close enough to their host star may experience tidal locking. Tidal locking can occur when the gravitational force exerted by the star induces tidal bulges on the planet. Over long periods of time torque caused by frictional forces within the planet conflict with the tidal stretching, which can cause the planet's rotational period to become synchronous with its orbital period (Barnes 2017). This results in the planet orbiting with one side continuously facing the star in a similar manner as the Moon rotates around the Earth. The impact of one side of the planet receiving constant stellar radiation and the other side receiving none could result in extreme weather conditions and variations between the day- and night-side of the planet that could have an effect on the evolution of life. Preliminary modeling of tidally locked planets and the effect it has on their atmospheres has taken place, but further characterization of the TRAPPIST-1 exoplanets will focus future research and lead us to better determine the potential for life on those planets (Barnes 2017).

5. Conclusions

Altogether, the study of exoplanets is a rather new and emerging field that has seen rapid breakthrough in the recent years but has great potential to be developed in the future. The number of new exoplanets being discovered is increasing every year, and as we develop better instrumentation we have the potential to identify many more exoplanets with methods that were not available when research first began. Additionally, planned projects such as the CHaracterizing ExOPlanet Satellite (CHEOPS) and the James Webb Space Telescope aim to study and characterize existing exoplanets in more detail as well as searching for new exoplanets.

As we are able to gather more details about exoplanets and better analyze their conditions, we can also learn much more about the conditions that make those planets habitable. Further research into what defines habitability has great potential in improving our overall understanding of life and the conditions that create it. Ultimately, as we continue researching exoplanets and potentially habitable worlds, we grow closer to being able to answer the questions at the core of astrobiological research and discover whether we are alone in the universe.

Works Cited:

Armstrong, J. C., Barnes, R., Domagal-Goldman, S., et al. 2014, Astrobiology, 14, 277, http://online.liebertpub.com/doi/abs/10.1089/ast.2013.1129

Barnes, R. 2017, Celest Mech Dyn Astron, 129, 509

Deeg, H. J., & Alonso, R. 2018, http://arxiv.org/abs/1803.07867

Fischer, D. A., Howard, A. W., Laughlin, G. P., et al. 2014, in Protostars and Planets VI, Vol. 1 (University of Arizona Press), 21, http://arxiv.org/abs/1306.2418

Gillon, M., Jehin, E., Lederer, S. M., et al. 2016, Nature, 533 (Nature Publishing Group), 221, http://dx.doi.org/10.1038/nature17448

Gillon, M., Triaud, A. H. M. J., Demory, B. O., et al. 2017, Nature, 542 (Nature Publishing Group), 456, http://dx.doi.org/10.1038/nature21360

Güdel, M., Dvorak, R., Erkaev, N., et al. 2014, in Protostars and Planets VI, Vol. 1 (University of Arizona Press), 21, http://arxiv.org/abs/1306.2418

Kasting, J. F., Whitmire, D. P., & Reynolds, R. T. 1993, Icarus, 101, 108, http://linkinghub.elsevier.com/retrieve/pii/S0019103583710109

Kopparapu, R. K., Ramirez, R., Kasting, J. F., et al. 2013, Astrophys J, 765

Des Marais, D. J., Nuth, J. A., Allamandola, L. J., et al. 2008, Astrobiology, 8, 715, http://www.liebertonline.com/doi/abs/10.1089/ast.2008.0819

Roettenbacher, R. M., & Kane, S. R. 2017, Astrophys J, 851 (IOP Publishing), 77, http://arxiv.org/abs/1711.02676%0Ahttp://dx.doi.org/10.3847/1538-4357/aa991e

Shields, A. L., Ballard, S., & Johnson, J. A. 2016, Phys Rep, 663 (Elsevier B.V.), 1, http://dx.doi.org/10.1016/j.physrep.2016.10.003

Wolszczan, A., & Frail, D. A. 1992, Nature, 355, 145, http://www.nature.com/doifinder/10.1038/355145a0

Wright, J. T. 2017, in Handbook of Exoplanets (Cham: Springer International Publishing), 1, http://arxiv.org/abs/1707.07983

Excellence in Upper-Level Writing (Social Sciences)

Best Strategies to Increase Public Support for a Tax on Sugar-Sweetened Beverages
by Samantha Goldstein
From PolSci381: Introduction to Research Design
Nominated by Aloka Narayanan (GSI), Nancy Burns (Faculty)

Samantha Goldstein submitted an original research proposal, "Best Strategies to Increase Public Support for a Tax on Sugar-Sweetened Beverages," as her final assignment in Political Science Research Design (PolSci 381) in Fall 2018. Samantha's research proposal not only exemplifies strong political science writing, but details research that promises to shed new light on public health policy interventions with broad societal implications. Through this proposal, she exhibits a thorough understanding of previous literature on the topic. Her research design is comprehensive and clear, and provides solid next steps for future work. I am confident this proposal sets her up to write a stellar honors thesis, that will contribute unique perspectives on Pigovian taxation framing to the field of Political Science.

Aloka Narayanan

Best Strategies to Increase Public Support for a Tax on Sugar-Sweetened Beverages

Introduction

The United States is in the midst of a battle against a particularly nefarious and expensive health crisis. As of 2016, the obesity epidemic afflicted 39.8% of US adults and nearly 20% of youth aged 6-11 years (Hales et al. 2017, 1). Minorities and low-income individuals suffer disproportionately from obesity. The prevalence of obesity is 47% for Hispanics and 46.8% for blacks compared to 37.9% for whites. 39% of low-income groups are obese compared to 31.2% for high-income groups (Ogden et al. 2017, 1371). This disparity is especially pronounced for women who have an obesity prevalence rate of 45.2% for the lowest income groups compared to 29.7% for the highest. Obesity is a highly comorbid disease: obese Americans are more likely to have Type II diabetes, insulin resistance, respiratory issues, heart disease, and psychological problems (Khaodhiar, McCowen, and Blackburn 1999, 19). Moreover, healthcare costs for obese individuals are $1,429 higher per year with most of the costs coming from private tax-payers (Finkelstein et al. 2009, w828). Without proper intervention, obesity rates will continue to rise and America will become fatter and sicker than ever.

Lawmakers and researchers have proposed a number of solutions to combat obesity with particular attention to decreasing the consumption of fattening and unhealthy foods. These solutions range from implementing stricter nutritional standards in schools to imposing taxes on sugar-sweetened beverages to disincentivize their purchase. The soda tax controversy pits individual food sovereignty against public health. Opponents of the soda tax argue the government has no right to selectively punish a legal product. However, the government already levies steep taxes on alcohol and cigarettes to promote reduced consumption in the name of public health. Jonathan Gruber (2010) at the Massachusetts Institute of Technology found that smokers are sensitive to price increases in cigarettes, decreasing consumption by 10% for each 10% rise in price. Similarly, Gruber determines a tax of 80 cents per ounce of pure alcohol serves as the baseline for combating the negative externalities of excess alcohol consumption. Still, taxation on food and beverages is much more personal; food taxes can be especially burdensome on low-income individuals who are more vulnerable to poor nutrition and obesity (FRAC). Regardless, the physical, emotional, and financial consequences of obesity do not live in isolation. Thus, it would behoove policymakers to consider imposing excise taxes on sugary beverages to thwart obesity and its associated medical costs.

Taxation specifically on food and drink has become especially controversial in the past couple decades. The idea of a tax on sugary beverages gained traction in the mid-90s with Dr. Kelly D. Brownell of the Rudd Center for Food Policy and Obesity at the University of Connecticut (previously at Yale University) proposing a "sin tax" on low-nutrition foods to reduce consumption and subsequently raise revenue for public exercise facilities or nutrition education in schools (Brownell 1994, A29). While the United States does not currently have a federal soda tax, a number of cities have passed their own versions of soda taxes. In 2014, the city of Berkeley, California became the first US jurisdiction to unanimously vote in favor of a one cent per ounce tax on the distributors of specific sugar-sweetened beverages (SSBs) including soda, sports drinks, energy drinks, and sweetened iced teas (Ballotpedia.org 2014). The Berkeley soda tax decreased consumption of SSBs by 21% in two large, low-income neighborhoods comprised mostly of minorities.

Although a soda tax is certainly not the solution to America's obesity epidemic, it offers a promising start. Theories in behavioral economics evince how changes in micro-behavior influence macro phenomenon such as obesity levels or measures of health. The soda industry is vociferous in its opposition to soda taxes (Nestle 2017). This thesis will demonstrate whether a countervailing message in support of a soda tax can resonate. For a soda tax policy to be enacted, political leaders must be convinced of one of two things: one, that there is some level of public support for it, or, two, that more public support for it can be generated. Even if a proposed piece of legislation is a good public policy, public support is imperative to get it passed due to the power of industry lobbyists and opposing interest groups. Thus, my thesis will illuminate the best strategies for generating public support for this tax.

Literature Review

In this literature review, I will begin with an analysis on the state of soda politics in the US and the argument for this tax. I will then discuss the literature on political communication and psychology with special emphasis on the technique of framing. Additionally, I will review the research on affective intelligence and political judgment based on exposure to different emotional cues. This review will provide valuable guidance in designing a campaign to encourage public support for state and federal soda taxes.

Soda Politics

The soda industry—comprised of the companies themselves (e.g., Coca-Cola and PepsiCo) and their associated trade association, the American Beverage Association, are exceptionally good at staying on message and deterring legislation that would threaten their profits. NYU Nutrition Professor, Marion Nestle (2017) outlines four tactics the soda industry uses to deflect their part in the obesity crisis: 1) emphasizing their devotion to health and wellness which includes diverting attention to physical activity's role in decreasing obesity rates, 2) heavy marketing and advertising of their products, 3) building allies through philanthropy efforts and partnering with health groups to bolster their public image, and 4) taking strong action to protect corporate interests. The soda industry is notorious for their inconsistent production and sales figures. Nevertheless, Grand View Research estimated the global carbonated beverage market's total worth at over $340 billion dollars in 2014.

Historically, the soda industry has fought proposed soda taxes by launching vigorous counter-offensive campaigns. Nestle (2017) equates Big Soda's response to tax proposals to that of the cigarette industry since both deflect attention away from the hazards of consuming their respective products. Both industries spend millions of dollars on these efforts ranging from lobbying policymakers to strike down tax proposals to blatantly lying about the role excess soda consumption plays in the obesity epidemic (Nestle 2017).

Even more nefarious are Big Soda's marketing efforts towards America's most vulnerable populations such as children, minorities, and low-income individuals. According to the UConn Rudd Center for Food Policy & Obesity (2014, 8), beverage companies spent a stunning $866 million on advertising sugary and energy drinks in the year 2013 alone. Advertisements for these drinks constituted two-thirds of all beverage advertisements viewed by children (9). Beverage advertising has transcended the classic mediums of television and print to also dominate social media. Soda companies use celebrities and popular music to increase their brand presence; they also host promotions and contests to engage younger users across various social media platforms such as Facebook, Twitter, YouTube, and Instagram (10).

The soda industry's marketing towards children toes the lines of what constitutes ethical advertising. Children are particularly vulnerable to the flashy advertising tactics of Big Soda. Black and Hispanic youth are subject to an increased risk of obesity, diabetes, hypertension, and other diet-related diseases, so aggressive advertising to these communities is especially troubling (Hales et al. 2017, 4).

A soda tax is just one of many solutions to combat America's obesity epidemic and addiction to sugar. The effectiveness of taxation on behavior change is rather persuasive. Kristensen et al. (2014, 606) determined that a sugar-sweetened beverage excise tax would, on average, decrease consumption by 35% for adolescents. The rationale for the tax follows the basic laws of supply and demand: as the price of soda rises, people will reduce their consumption, and ideally, obesity rates will fall. Wright et al. (2017) argue a health tax that increases the price of products by 20% would reduce consumption. As aforementioned, a number of American localities have implemented small taxes—typically one to one-and-a-half cents per ounce—and found significant drops in soda consumption while simultaneously raising millions of dollars in revenue (Andreyeva et al. 2011).[1] Wang et al. (2012) determined a penny-per-ounce excise tax on SSBs would discourage consumption by 6-24% among adults ages 25-64 and over the course of ten years result in 95,000 fewer instances of coronary heart disease, 8,000 fewer strokes, and 26,000 fewer premature deaths. Beyond the health effects, such a tax would save over $17 billion in medical expenditures to fight obesity and its associated health ramifications like type 2 diabetes. In sum, the SSB tax is an effective example of a Pigouvian taxation aimed at decreasing the costs of sugary tax consumption.

Framing and Persuasion Theory

Framing is fundamental to understanding persuasion. Although a precise definition of framing has yet to be cemented, Jamie Druckman (2001, 227), an expert on political preference formation and communication, describes it as a mixture of the words, images, phrases, and presentation styles that a speaker uses to relay information, as well as the issues a speaker sees as relevant and thus warrant emphasis (Cappella and Jamieson 1997, Gamson and Modigliani 1987, Gitlin 1980, Iyengar 1991). The literature on framing is extensive. To best understand framing, one must also consider citizen competence in the context of heuristics, information shortcuts and the effects of elite manipulation (Lupia and McCubbins 1998). Druckman (2001) outlines two notions of framing: *frames in communication* and *frames in thought*. A frame in communication often "draws on a person's goals and values in order to state a view on a contested issue" (29). Thus, frames in communication could include an "economy frame" utilized by a politician to make economic issues more prominent in the minds of voters. The second frame, *frames in thought*, describes how an individual perceives a situation. These frames in thought serve as the basis for decision-making.

---

1 For a twelve-ounce can of regular soda, this would mean a twelve cents tax or a 15-25% increase in price.

For the purpose of this literature review, I will focus on the technique of emphasis framing which alters overall opinions to make certain considerations more salient in the minds of respondents (Druckman 2001, 231). The perennial example of emphasis framing refers to a Ku Klux Klan rally being framed as a free speech event that should be allowed to proceed versus a dangerous event threatening public safety (Nelson, Clawson, and Oxley 1997).

In the context of my research on generating support for a tax on soda, the importance of framing cannot be understated. Taxation is already a polarizing topic due to its personally meddlesome nature. Thus, framing such an unattractive policy in a positive, necessary light poses a formidable challenge. Framing's effectiveness relies heavily on citizen competence—or lack thereof. On the outset, a number of potential frames for marketing a soda tax come to mind such as a public health crisis frame that contextualizes the tax in the greater obesity epidemic. On the other hand, the frame could stray away from fear-mongering and instead use a lighter, more encouraging frame about the virtues of water over SSBs.

A whole subfield of political science dedicated to evaluating the effects of framing within political domains also exists. Policy framing research has historically used the technique of equivalency framing which examines how different, but logically equivalent words and phrases lead to preference formation (Druckman 2001, 228). For example, describing the economy as having 95% employment versus 5% unemployment. Typically the frames used take positive and negative positions with one frame being more effective in generating the expected response. Equivalency framing is not simply limited to the political sphere, but is ubiquitous in everyday life. Food companies are notorious for framing their products as 97% fat-free, but a label advertising a food as containing the equivalent 3% fat might actually discourage consumers from purchasing it. On the other hand, frames are constantly exploited to promote a certain side of a polarizing political issue like abortion with its pro-choice versus pro-life labels where each consciously attempts to activate certain morals and ethics (Druckman 2001, 228).

With regards to policy framing, an experiment conducted by Paul Brewer (2007) used media frames emphasizing either equality or morality to measure support for gay rights. After controlling for confounding variables, Brewer discovered that an equality frame led to more support for gay rights, while a morality frame had the opposite effect. Shanto Iyengar (1991) expands on the framing literature to distinguish between episodic and thematic frames. Episodic themes refer to individual stories such as one family's struggle to pay their bills, while thematic frames are more general and focus on societal patterns like increases in poverty nationwide. Frame strength depends on how credible the source is, and also whether it is episodic or thematic (Busby, Flynn, and Druckman 2018, 28). In general, Lene Aarøe (2011) determined episodic frames are stronger than thematic frames since they evoke more of an emotional response from participants due to the personal nature of the frame. In my research, I plan to evaluate the efficacy of each type of frame on generating public support for a tax on soda.

Affective Intelligence and Emotional Cues

Previous social science research has mainly focused on generally understanding how emotional appeals elicit certain feelings in viewers. However, in political science, this research has been mostly limited to candidate and campaign ads, rather than ads related to policy proposals (see Neuman 2007, Brader 2006). This thesis will add a new perspective to the field by analyzing how advertisements appealing to specific emotions can impact the public image of a tangible piece of legislation.

In their book, *Affective Intelligence and Political Judgement*, Marcus, Neuman, and MacKuen (2000) introduce the theory of Affective Intelligence which at its most basic level states that emotions attached to politics are dynamic in that they have both state (contemporary) and trait (permanent) characteristics. By eliciting certain emotions, actors in the political sphere can galvanize predictable responses in citizens (65). Furthermore, Marcus and his colleagues introduce the concept of a surveillance system that monitors the environment for "novel and threatening stimuli" (53). Surveillance acts as a subconscious emotional process that has far-reaching effects on habit change and behavior. The authors argue that in addition to provoking behavior change, the surveillance system also invokes greater attentiveness, thoughtfulness, and an increased desire for learning. Applying the surveillance system to politics presents a prime opportunity for persuasion. When an individual is exposed to anxious conditions, three things can occur simultaneously: one, people no longer rely on their political habits, two, there is an increased motivation to learn more information, and third, people can be persuaded to adopt alternative views resulting from their increased open-mindedness (Marcus, Neuman, and MacKuen 2000, 53). In sum, an anxious voter is more pliable to engaging with substitute views.

Subsequent research by Ted Brader (2006) applies the theory of affective intelligence to evaluate how distinct emotional cues such as enthusiasm, fear, and anxiety provoke certain responses in citizens and either encourage or discourage information-seeking. In general, enthusiasm is more closely related to reinforcing previously held views over persuasion; Brader argues enthusiasm is an appropriate cue for "rallying the faithful" where the faithful enjoy greater political knowledge. On the other hand, fear and anxiety cues should alarm inattentive citizens and pave the way for persuasion. For negative affective appraisals—namely anxiety and aversion—the general consensus is that those emotional cues stimulating anxiety are more conducive to compromise and cooperation over those that stimulate anger or aversion (MacKuen et al. 2010, 442).

Public Preferences & the Role of Interest Groups

Legislative action is directly related to the confluence of legislator and public preference (Arnold 1992). Miller and Stokes (1963) associate constituency influence with three conditions: first, that policymakers vote according to their own views and the views of their constituents, second, that the attitudes governing the policymakers' actions correspond to what their districts actually want, and third, that the constituencies take the policymakers' views into account when voting them into office. In general, the constituency's attitude, the representative's attitude, the representative's perception of the constituency's attitude, and the representative's roll call behavior should be more or less intercorrelated.

In order to be re-elected, members of Congress must reflect the views and policy preferences of their constituents (Arnold 1992). Accordingly, if public support for a tax on soda, for example, is high enough, it would behoove the member of Congress to vote in favor of it. A vote aligning with the public's preference bolsters the representative's reputation, positioning him for a successful re-election bid. Legislative decision-making also depends on the salience of an issue. In other words, legislators need to know if their vote on a policy will resonate with the electorate or isolate them instead.

To reiterate the necessity of public support in passing new legislation, it is important to emphasize the point that sufficient public support for such a policy does not imply a "reward" for the Congressman or woman who votes for it. It only implies that he or she will not be punished for it, i.e., losing their seat.

While persuasive, the theory that a legislator's views and actions reflect those of his or her constituents becomes complicated when organized interests get involved. Interest groups strive to shape legislator perceptions about the consequences of their votes or actions (Arnold 1992). When it comes to the soda tax, opposing interest groups actively work to convince members that supporting such a tax would have negative electoral consequences—whether that is true or not. My thesis will examine whether and what sort of messages can be developed to counteract the arguments of such anti-soda tax actors.

In the context of passing a proposed policy through the legislation, both public support and interest group support are imperative. In addition to money, there are several other ways interest groups can strike down legislation they prefer not to pass. These include mass mobilization efforts like stimulating constituents to contact their member of Congress and encourage he or she votes against the proposed legislation (35). Interest groups are quite successful at increasing issue salience which is conducive to a proposal's success or failure (38). Therefore, any strategy for increasingly popular support for a tax on soda, per se, would have to take into account outside influence. Conversely, supporters of such a tax could recruit interest and advocacy groups in favor of these interventional public health measures to combat the actions of anti-soda tax interest groups.[2]

Research Design

Soda taxes in the United States have thus far been generally unsuccessful in either getting passed or avoiding getting repealed. According to the UConn Rudd Center for Food Policy and Obesity, between 2010 and November 2018, 172 bills regarding taxing sugar-sweetened beverages (SSBs) were introduced to state legislatures along with three federal bills. Of those, seven passed with the remaining bills either failing, dying in committee, or being ordered for "further study" (i.e., dying). One reason for the failures is a lack of overall public support. A 2011 public opinion survey found greater agreement with anti-tax arguments over pro-tax ones (Barry, Niederdeppe, and Gollust 2013). 60% felt a tax on SSBs was arbitrary since it did not affect the consumption of other unhealthy food (159). 53.8% felt the tax was an unacceptable intrusion by the government into citizens' private lives, and 53% opposed the tax generally. None of the pro-tax arguments sustained a majority of public support. Nevertheless, Barry and her colleagues argue that public support for the tax could still be generated with the appropriate messaging technique. In particular, they suggest advocates of the tax emphasize research evidence that SSBs are the largest contributors to obesity, enunciating how revenue from the tax would go towards obesity prevention. They claim these strategies would make the policy more "politically palatable" and therefore, easier to pass through the legislature (161).

My research question seeks to fill existing gaps in the literature about how to most effectively make a case for taxes on sugar-sweetened beverages including non-diet sodas, sports drinks, and energy drinks. The dependent variable is overall support for the tax which will be measured through a variety of survey questions

---

2 The pro-tax interest groups would most likely include organizations dedicated to improving public health such as the World Health Organization, the American Heart Association, and the Nutrition Science Initiative. On the contrary, the anti-tax interest groups would certainly comprise industry organizations such as the American Beverage Association and potentially libertarian organizations against encroachments on personal freedoms.

designed to measure both implicit and explicit attitudes. For instance, after the experiment, an open-ended question might prompt respondents to recount which messaging tactic they felt was the most persuasive to them. On the other hand, there will be a variety of questions for each strategy with questions aimed at discovering the ideal tax rate which will both maximize public support while still disincentivizing the consumption of these beverages.

I plan to conduct two experiments in stages: one will be a classic survey experiment with message testing batteries and split-half questions, while the second will expose respondents to print and television content eliciting a variety of emotional cues. Both experiments will be held on the same online platform. For the first experiment, the independent variables will be several frames of pro-tax arguments. I will base these arguments off the ones Barry, Niederdeppe, and Gollust used in the survey mentioned above such as how sodas are the largest driver of the obesity crisis versus an argument emphasizing how a penny-per-ounce soda tax would raise $150 billion over 10 years to combat childhood obesity (160). This will allow me to ascertain which particular arguments resonate the most with respondents. For example, some respondents may identify more with the public health rationale for a soda tax while others might find the financial rationale more persuasive.

For the first experiment, my primary hypothesis is that framing the soda tax as the most effective solution to curb skyrocketing obesity rates will galvanize the most support out of all the arguments. Emphasizing sugar's role as a public health threat should trigger anxiety which Affective Intelligence Theory posits is the most conducive to compromise and cooperation (MacKuen et al. 2010, 442). An alternative hypothesis is that the economic frame of the SSB tax, specifically that the $150 billion revenue resulting from the tax could be used for programs preventing childhood obesity, would instead be the most effective.

My second experiment involves exposing participants to print and TV campaigns for the soda tax using various message-framing techniques designed to elicit specific emotions such as anxiety, fear, or enthusiasm. My dependent variable will not change from the first experiment; I am still interested in measuring overall support for the tax, yet this time, my independent variables will be the physical print and TV advertisements. Each will use a variety of framing techniques and emotional cues to evaluate the relative effectiveness of that particular strategy. Building off research on political psychology, framing, and emotional cues, I hypothesize a media campaign stimulating anxiety will be the most effective in generating support for this tax. Affective Intelligence Theory and the research on political issue frames are rather persuasive in arguing that anxiety increases information-seeking relevant to the decision at hand and that it also decreases attachment to predispositions or prior attitudes (Brader and Marcus 2013). In practice, a messaging technique using anxiety may take the form of a campaign highlighting soda's role in the obesity epidemic. An alternative hypothesis is that a strategy emphasizing the need for a soda tax through an anger lens will be the most compelling in garnering public support. In general, I hypothesize a message campaign portraying soda as a threat will be the most compelling for viewers.

To measure my dependent variable of support for the soda tax, I plan to ask respondents a series of questions both before and after exposing them to the pro-tax campaigns. Before exposure, I will prompt respondents to answer questions about taxation in general, the specific SSB tax, and demographic questions so I can control for party identification and other attributes that may affect an answer. For the questions on opinions for the tax, I plan to use Likert Scale questions which are more nuanced and easily quantifiable. For instance, one question could prompt respondents to rank how much they agree with the following statement, "A tax on non-diet sodas, sports drinks, and energy drinks would lead to lower consumption and better health." from *Strongly Disagree* to *Strongly Agree*. Whereas other questions could solicit more personal opinions where political leanings are more clearly illuminated such as "A soda tax is an overreach of government into the lives and choices of private citizens." I will base the language off Barry, Niederdeppe, and Gollust's 2011 national public opinion survey assessing attitudes regarding SSB taxes (160).

Additionally, the survey will also pose a handful of open-ended questions to solicit further information about why a person might be for or against a soda tax. These questions might take the form, "How do you feel, generally, about a penny-per-ounce tax on sugar-sweetened beverages?" or "Besides taxation, what are some other policies the US could adopt to fight the obesity epidemic?" These questions should also evince a person's political leanings which are likely to cloud their views on interventionist government policies like a soda tax. I plan to partner with experienced survey designers to ensure my experiment and questionnaire follows standard survey protocol.

After exposing the viewer to a particular messaging strategy using randomization software, I will prompt the respondent to answer questions ascertaining their attitudes towards both the campaign and the overarching tax it advertised. Once again, I plan to use a mix of Likert Scale questions and open-ended questions to establish what kind of causal role—if any—the emotional appeal played on generating public support for the SSB tax. Post-treatment, I plan to also pose a series of questions aimed at determining if a particular emotional cue was salient. For example, one question might propel the respondent to choose from a list of emotions about how the framed messaging campaign made them feel: angry, fearful, anxious, enthusiastic, rational, etc. Indeed, experiments related to political psychology are more challenging for determining causality due to the complex nature of how humans process information. Isolating responses to emotional, political phenomena is still relatively uncharted territory. However, I will base my survey design off those from eminent and reliable researchers in the field of political psychology and media such as Ted Brader, Nicholas Valentino, and Don Kinder at the University of Michigan and Shanto Iyengar at Stanford University.

I hope to conduct my survey on a higher-quality platform that uses a more representative sample. The first option is to conduct telephone polling using SSRS Omnibus. This is a high-quality telephone omnibus (65 percent cell phone/35 percent landline) poll that uses probability sampling. The omnibus runs

Wednesday through Sunday each week. The cost is $1,100-1,500 per question for 1,000 respondents and includes breakdowns by age, race, education, gender, and party identification, as well as other basic demographics. This poll is a cost-efficient way for me to evaluate how various messages influence attitudes towards the soda tax. Also, because this is a probability sample, I can use it to benchmark and compare results from other non-probability samples I may use due to budget constraints.

The second option is to conduct an online poll using SurveyMonkey. Through this technology, I will conduct experiments to determine which messages or creatives work best with different sub-groups. If I test actual content, I will do this in two stages: testing rough cuts first, and then testing to tweak more finished products. The SurveyMonkey panel will be core to this work. This panel uses non-probability river sampling drawn from the millions of respondents who complete SurveyMonkey surveys in a typical month.

A probability sample would be ideal, albeit more expensive. Since I am conducting an experiment, probability samples are less important. However, depending on if I can secure a Gerstein grant, it may make sense to invest in the higher quality platform. To carry out my analyses, I will use R to create confidence intervals for the population mean level of support each messaging technique generates. Since I will mainly be relying on Likert Scale data, I will also conduct an ordinal regression using the *ordinal* package in R which offers a powerful framework for experimental designs such as mine. I plan to meet with consultants at U-M's Center for Statistical Consultation and Research (CSCAR) in developing my R script and conducting the subsequent analyses.

In terms of measurement errors, I worry about accurately measuring the outcome variables, i.e., gauging someone's true tolerance for a soda tax. Respondents may feel differently about their support for a tax in the abstract versus when it is actually implemented. Additionally, it is possible that the emotional cues and frames used in my experiment will not be immediately salient to the respondent, and thus, my independent variable will be ineffective. This is why I plan to include a "neutral" response option in my survey. In any experiment, it is crucial to guard against response bias and demand characteristics. Throughout the research design process, I plan to consult with seasoned researchers familiar with reconciling these potential issues. Brader (2006) acknowledges these limitations in his own experiments on emotions in political life cautioning that "the capacity to elicit particular emotions may be highly sensitive to prevailing conditions and concerns." Thus, in my experiment, I plan to gather a more holistic picture of who is in my sample by asking demographic questions which will allow me to control for particular pre-dispositions or attitudes towards a soda tax.

Conclusion

An issue as polarizing as sin taxation poses a fascinating domain to study. Public health measures are in constant conflict with notions of individual freedom central to the American spirit. Generating support for such an inherently unattractive tax on sugar-sweetened beverages is a formidable challenge. My research evaluating which frame is the most effective for garnering support for a soda tax can be applied to various other measures such as cigarettes, alcohol, or even unhealthy food—all of which have taxes currently in place or embroiled in the legislative process. This thesis occupies the intersection of political science, economics, and psychology. At the end of my research, I hope to find two things: one, that it is possible to generate a majority of support for a soda tax through effective framing, and two, to find which specific frame that is. In the meantime, I will continue to hone my survey research skills through Professor Valentino's POLSCI 499: Survey Design course and the methodological workshops offered by ICPSR over the summer. I will also continue reading the literature on framing techniques and persuasion.

The concept of dynamic representation proposed by Stimson, Mackuen, and Erikson (1995) describes how public policy responds to shifts in public opinion. Historical precedent supports the claim that politicians do in fact translate changes in public opinion into tangible policy change (559). In the context of my research, public support is crucial for a tax on sugar-sweetened beverages to pass the legislature. Legislators must see that a vote in favor of the SSB tax will not threaten their chances for re-election. The sugar and soda industries will continue to win so long as nobody effectively messages on the other side. My thesis will illuminate how a persuasive, countervailing message in favor of a tax on soda can gain the support of both legislators and the equally integral public. A salient frame advocating for an SSB tax has the potential to embolden both supporters and indifferent individuals. In doing so, the politicians ultimately voting on such a policy will be more inclined to vote in favor of it. Ultimately, it is the public that will decide the fate of this tax.

Bibliography

Aarøe, Lene. "Investigating frame strength: The case of episodic and thematic frames." *Political Communication* 28, no. 2 (2011): 207-226.

Arnold, R. Douglas. *The logic of congressional action.* Yale University Press, 1992.

Barry, Colleen L., Jeff Niederdeppe, Sarah E. Gollust, Taxes on Sugar-Sweetened Beverages: Results from a 2011 National Public Opinion Survey, American Journal of Preventive Medicine, Volume 44, Issue 2, 2013, Pages 158-163, ISSN 0749-3797, https://doi.org/10.1016/j.amepre.2012.09.065.

Brader, Ted. *Campaigning for Hearts and Minds: How Emotional Appeals in Political Ads Work.* Chicago, IL: University of Chicago Press, 2006.

Brader, Ted, and George E. Marcus. "Emotion and Political Psychology." In *The Oxford Handbook of Political Psychology.* : Oxford University Press, 2013-09-04. http://www.oxfordhandbooks.com/view/10.1093/oxfordhb/9780199760107.001.0001/oxfordhb-9780199760107-e-006.

Brewer, Paul R. *Value war: Public opinion and the politics of gay rights.* Rowman & Littlefield Publishers, 2007.

Brownell, Kelly D. "Get slim with higher taxes." *New York Times* 15 (1994): A29.

Cappella, Joseph N., and Jamieson, Kathleen Hall (1997). *Spiral of Cynicism: The Press and the Public Good*. New York: Oxford University Press.

"Carbonated Beverages Market Analysis, Market Size, Application Analysis, Regional Outlook, Competitive Strategies, and Forecasts, 2015 To 2022." Personalized Medicine Market Analysis By Product And Segment Forecasts To 2022. Accessed November 10, 2018. https://www.grandviewresearch.com/industry-analysis/carbonated-beverages-market.

"City of Berkeley Sugary Beverages and Soda Tax Question, Measure D (November 2014)." Ballotpedia. Accessed November 10, 2018. https://ballotpedia.org/City_of_Berkeley_Sugary_Beverages_and_Soda_Tax_Question,_Measure_D_(November_2014).

Druckman, James N. "The implications of framing effects for citizen competence." *Political behavior* 23, no. 3 (2001): 225-256.

Finkelstein, Eric A., Justin G. Trogdon, Joel W. Cohen, and William Dietz. "Annual medical spending attributable to obesity: payer-and service-specific estimates." *Health affairs* 28, no. 5 (2009): w822-w831.

Gamson, William A.,and Modigliani,Andre (1987).The changing culture of affirmative action. In Richard D.Braungart (ed.), *Research in Political Sociology*, vol.3, pp.137–177.Greenwich,CT: JAI.

Gitlin, Todd (1980). *The Whole World Is Watching:Mass Media in the Making & Unmaking of the New Left*. Berkeley: University of California Press.

Gruber, Jonathan. "Taxing Sin to Modify Behavior and Raise Revenue." *Expert Voices NIHCM* 55 (2010).

Hales CM, Carroll MD, Fryar CD, Ogden CL. Prevalence of obesity among adults and youth: United States, 2015–2016. NCHS data brief, no 288.

Hyattsville, MD: National Center for Health Statistics. 2017.

Iyengar, Shanto (1991). *Is Anyone Responsible?: How Television Frames Political Issues*. Chicago: The University of Chicago Press.

Jou, Judy, Jeff Niederdeppe, Colleen L. Barry, and Sarah E. Gollust. "Strategic messaging to promote taxation of sugar-sweetened beverages: Lessons from recent political campaigns." *American Journal of Public Health* 104, no. 5 (2014): 847-853.

Khaodhiar, Lalita, Karen C. McCowen, and George L. Blackburn. "Obesity and its comorbid conditions." *Clinical cornerstone* 2, no. 3 (1999): 17-31.

Kristensen, Alyson H., Thomas J. Flottemesch, Michael V. Maciosek, Jennifer Jenson, Gillian Barclay, Marice Ashe, Eduardo J. Sanchez, Mary Story, Steven M. Teutsch, and Ross C. Brownson. "Reducing childhood obesity through US federal policy: a microsimulation analysis." *American journal of preventive medicine* 47, no. 5 (2014): 604-612.

Lupia, Arthur, and McCubbins, Mathew D. (1998). The Democratic Dilemma: Can Citizens Learn What They Need To Know? New York: Cambridge University Press.

"Legislation Database - Tracks Policies Related to Obesity." Food Marketing - UConn Rudd Center for Food Policy and Obesity. Accessed November 15, 2018. http://www.uconnruddcenter.org/legislation-database.

MacKuen, Michael, Jennifer Wolak, Luke Keele, and George E. Marcus. "Civic engagements: Resolute partisanship or reflective deliberation." *American Journal of Political Science* 54, no. 2 (2010): 440-458.

Marcus, George E., W. Russell. Neuman, and Michael Bruce. MacKuen. *Affective Intelligence and Political Judgement*. Chicago: University of Chicago Press, 2000.

Miller, Warren E., and Donald E. Stokes. "Constituency influence in Congress." *American political science review* 57, no. 1 (1963): 45-56.

Mytton, Oliver T., Dushy Clarke, and Mike Rayner. "Taxing unhealthy food and drinks to improve health." *BMJ: British Medical Journal (Online)* 344 (2012).

Nelson, Thomas E., Rosalee A. Clawson, and Zoe M. Oxley. "Media framing of a civil liberties conflict and its effect on tolerance." *American Political Science Review* 91, no. 3 (1997): 567-583.

Nestle, Marion. *Soda Politics: Taking on Big Soda (and Winning)*. Oxford: Oxford University Press, 2017.

Neuman, W. Russell. *The Affect Effect: Dynamics of Emotion in Political Thinking and Behavior*. Chicago: Univ. of Chicago Press, 2007.

Ogden CL, Fakhouri TH, Carroll MD, et al. Prevalence of Obesity Among Adults, by Household Income and Education — United States, 2011–2014. MMWR Morb Mortal Wkly Rep 2017;66:1369–1373. DOI: http://dx.doi.org/10.15585/mmwr.mm6650a1.

Stimson, J. A., Mackuen, M. B., & Erikson, R. S. (1995). Dynamic representation. *American Political Science Review, 89*(3), 543-565. https://doi.org/10.2307/2082973.

"Why Low-Income and Food-Insecure People Are Vulnerable to Poor Nutrition and Obesity." Food Research & Action Center. Accessed November 10, 2018. http://frac.org/obesity-health/low-income-food-insecure-people-vulnerable-poor-nutrition-obesity.

Excellence in Upper-Level Writing (Social Sciences)

Colonialism and Environmental Discrimination in the Asia-Pacific: The US military in Guam and Okinawa
by Henry Schnaidt

From AAS322/Environ 335: Introduction to Environmental Politics
Nominated by Omolade Adunbi

In this essay, Henry critically analyzed the development of overseas US military bases and their social, environmental, and political implications. He further argued that these military bases can be interpreted as a 20th and 21st-century resurgence of colonialism. After extensively researching the subject, Henry identified an important gap in the existing literature- that current definitions of colonialism and neo-colonialism do not accurately reflect the trend of developing overseas military bases and their social and environmental impacts. In response to this gap, he proposed an alternative theoretical framework with which to explain this phenomenon - military/base colonialism. Henry deeply explores this topic and develops a comprehensive and compelling argument for his proposed theory. This reflects the nuanced approach and the critical thought Henry used to develop a robust and well-defended argument. Henry's paper is not only strongly grounded in the relevant theory which he deftly applies to his argument, but his paper is also written in an engaging way that hooks the reader in until the very end.

Adunbi Omolade

Colonialism and Environmental Discrimination in the Asia-Pacific: The US military in Guam and Okinawa

Not including the 50 states and the District of Columbia, the United States Military currently owns, leases, or joint-operates over 800 overseas bases (Vine, 2017). These bases are spread across more than 70 nations, including Iraq, Afghanistan, South Korea, and Germany, as well as in many perhaps less-familiar locations such as Honduras, Kenya, and Oman (Vine, 2015 and 2017). In terms of the sheer number of troops and volume of equipment however, the Asia-Pacific region has one of the highest concentrations of US forces in the world. Combined, the US Army, Marine Corps, Navy, and Air Force have approximately 375,000 soldiers and civilians stationed in the region, along with approximately 200 ships and around 2,460 aircraft ("About United States Indo-Pacific Command," 2018). These forces are divided primarily between bases in Japan, South Korea, and Guam, with additional forces said to be stationed in the Northern Mariana Islands, the Marshall Islands, the Philippines, Thailand, and Singapore (Holmes, 2017; Vine, 2017).

Thanks to the acquisition of Guam from Spain at the end of the Spanish-American War in 1898, US involvement in the Asia-Pacific dates back more than a century (Lutz, 2017). It was not until World War II and after that US involvement in the region began to approach what it is today, however. Guam was retaken by US troops in 1944, while the southern-most Japanese island chain of Okinawa was taken at great cost in 1945 (Lutz, 2017). Following the war, several large US military bases were established on Guam and Okinawa and subsequently used as stopping-off points and staging areas for the Korean War, the Vietnam War, and eventually the wars in Iraq and Afghanistan (Babauta, 2018; Inoue et al., 1998). During the Cold War with the Soviet Union, these bases and others throughout the region were seen as key to the US policy of containment (De Castro, 1994). After the fall of the Soviet Union in 1989, the focus of US policy shifted towards the deterrence of North Korea and the containment of China as an emerging power rivaling that of the US in East Asia (De Castro, 1994). Over the years, a key motivating factor behind US policy in the Asia-Pacific region has been ensuring access to Asia's markets through the maintenance of open shipping lanes and preventing the domination of another (military) power in the region (De Castro, 1994; Lutz, 2017). As such, US soldiers continue to deploy to bases in both Guam and Okinawa in large numbers.

There is no doubt that the US military's occupation of bases across the Asia-Pacific region has had a tremendous effect on the people living around these bases, especially in terms of the environment, but in terms of cultural, social, economic, and political impacts as well. In Guam and Okinawa in particular, such issues include a loss of access to land, the danger and nuisance of constant military operations (especially those involving military aircraft), increased levels of crime by US servicemembers (including rape and murder), and the detrimental health effects of environmental contamination. In light of these ills, environmental and otherwise, the US military's presence in the Asia-Pacific, and in particular in Guam and Okinawa, represents a new form of colonialism. This new colonialism is not traditional colonialism, as neither territory is under the direct political, economic, or cultural domination of the US (Wickens and Sandlin, 2007). Nor is it neocolonialism however, as neither Guam or Okinawa is under the direct exploitation of the global capitalist system (Condit and Kavoori, 1998).

Rather, the US military's presence in both Guam and Okinawa can be theorized as a "military base colonialism," in which a foreign power dominates a territory or nation through the housing of its armed forces in bases established on that territory or nation's land. In both Guam and Okinawa, this military base colonialism has taken place through a territorializing process of land control, carried out by the US government for the express purpose of constructing military bases and thereby establishing a military presence in the Asia-Pacific (Peluso and Lund, 2011). In turn, this process of territorialization has led to environmental discrimination by the US military in Guam and Okinawa (as well as in other locations in the Asia-Pacific region). By choosing to center its presence in the Asia-Pacific in Guam and Okinawa, the US military has disproportionately impacted communities in both locations based on race/ethnicity, culture, and socioeconomic status with environmental pollution and contamination from its bases and facilities.

Although war in and of itself is highly destructive to the environment, military bases can also be sources of environmental pollution and contamination. As one of the largest militaries in the world, the US military is also one of the world's largest polluters (Webb, 2017). Broadly, environmental pollution and degradation from military bases can result from two main elements: the construction and development of the base itself, and the day to day operations (including training) of the base (Lawrence et al., 2015). Common contaminants include fuels, oil, highly toxic pesticides such as Agent Orange (which contains the chemical dioxin), depleted uranium, PCBs, PFAS chemicals, and lead and other heavy metals such as mercury (Webb, 2017). Together, such pollutants seep into the soil underneath and surrounding military bases, eventually leaking into underground aquifers and contaminating drinking water supplies used by military personnel and the surrounding communities (Webb, 2017).

In Guam and Okinawa, such pollution and contamination has been a problem for decades. Geographically, the island of Guam is located in the South Pacific, due east of the Philippines and southeast of Japan and the two Koreas. At approximately 550 square kilometers in area, the island is quite small, with a population of about 160,000 people and a generally warm, tropical climate (Burrows, 2017). Guam is currently an unincorporated territory of the US (Babauta, 2018). The people of Guam, who include the indigenous Chamorro people (at around 40 percent of the population), along with a sizeable Filipino population, are US citizens, but cannot vote in US national elections or send voting representatives to US Congress (Burrows, 2017, "Guam Territory Profile," 2018). The island is run by an elected governor, and a 15-member senate (Burrows, 2017).

Guam was originally settled by the Chamorro people around 4,000 years ago (Burrows, 2017). After the island's discovery for the West by Ferdinand Magellan around 1521, Guam was claimed by Spain in 1565 ("Guam Territory Profile," 2018). With the Paris Treaty and the end of the Spanish-American War in 1898 however, control of Guam, along with the Philippines and Puerto Rico, was transferred to the US (Babauta, 2018). The island has remained under the control of the US ever since, except for a brief interlude from 1941-1944 during WWII when it was occupied by the Japanese (Lutz, 2017). After its reconquest by the US, Guam was used as a base for bombing raids on Japan (Babauta, 2018). After the war ended in 1945, the US military buildup on Guam began in earnest, with the construction of several military facilities. Much of the land on which these facilities were built was taken from the indigenous Chamorro people; land that the US military still controls to this day (Babauta, 2018). Throughout the decades then, Guam has functioned as an important base of operation for the wars in Korea, Vietnam, the Gulf, Iraq, and Afghanistan (Babauta, 2018).

Currently, the US military controls about one-third of the land on Guam (Babauta, 2018). The military's presence on the island is centered around Andersen Air Force Base in the north, and Naval Base Guam in Apra Harbor on the southwest side of the island, both of which are now combined as the Joint Region Marianas. Altogether, there are about 4,000 troops stationed on Guam, along with a full complement of fighter jets and bombers, as well as 4 nuclear-powered attack submarines and two submarine tenders (Burrows, 2017). In addition, Guam received a THAAD anti-ballistic missile battery in 2013 (Burrows, 2017).

For better or worse, the US military presence on Guam has become a part of the island's culture. Over the decades, Guam has had one of the highest military enlistment rates out of any of the US States and territories (Owen, 2010). In recent years however, a movement for self-governance has gained momentum (Yuen, 2017). This movement has been characterized by Chamorro protests over the continued military use of their ancestral lands, as well as a US military plan to relocate approximately 5,000 Marines to Guam from bases in Okinawa starting in 2020 (Babauta, 2018). Protests and anger over the presence of the US military have also been fueled by local fears regarding the designation of Guam as a potential missile target by North Korea (Babauta, 2018).

Finally, in addition to the issues mentioned above, environmental contamination from Guam's military bases has been a significant problem for the island over the years. Coastal waters around the island have been polluted from years of weapons testing (Yuen, 2017). On the land itself, both soil and groundwater below and surrounding US military facilities have most likely been polluted from the leakage of various chemicals and hazardous materials stored at these facilities. Such materials stored over the years include nuclear weapons, chemical weapons such as phosgene and mustard gas, various hazardous cleaning agents, carcinogenic insecticides and pesticides, as well as unexploded munitions (which not only pollute the environment but have the potential to cause serious injury or death as well) ("Toxic Bases in the Pacific," 2005). In one specific incident, a US submarine discharged nuclear waste water into Apra Bay in the late 1980s. More recently, several wells in and around Andersen AFB have been shut down due to groundwater contamination, most likely, but not necessarily from the base ("Toxic Bases in the Pacific," 2005).

High levels of pollution have been recorded at Andersen Air Force Base in particular. In 1992, the base was designated for cleanup as a (highly contaminated) Superfund site on the EPA's National Priorities List (Borja, 2017). Cleanup has been ongoing, albeit at a very slow pace, ever since. Hazardous materials implicated by the EPA in the cleanup include vaguely stated "operational solvents" ("Andersen Air Force Base Yigo, GU," EPA, 2018). Other materials include various cleaning fluids, pesticides, PCBs, and jet fuel (Borja, 2017). Sources of contamination may have included industrial activities as well as toxic waste dump sites. Initially, there were approximately 98 sites within the base specifically identified as needing cleanup (Borja, 2017). Many of these sites have since been decontaminated, but a significant number still have not. Contamination around the base is of particular concern given that it sits directly above the Northern Lens Aquifer, one of the main sources of drinking water for the entire island.

Like Guam, Okinawa is another island in the Asia-Pacific known for a large US military presence. Okinawa is the biggest island in the Ryukyu island chain, which extends from mainland Japan in the north almost to Taiwan in the south ("Ryukyu Islands," Encyclopedia Britannica, 2018). Part of Japan's southernmost Okinawa Prefecture, the island is 1,204 square kilometers in area, with a subtropical climate, and a population of about 1.85 million people (Denyer and Kashiwagi, 2018; "Ryukyu Islands," Encyclopedia Britannica, 2018).

Okinawa was once part of the independent Kingdom of Ryukyu, which had its own distinct language and culture, albeit with strong Chinese and Japanese influences, until it was formally annexed by Japan in 1879 (Bugni, 1997; Shorrock, 2005). Okinawa remained under Japanese control until 1945, when the US military invaded the island in one of the final battles of WWII. After the end of the war, the US continued to formally occupy and govern the island until 1972, a full 20 years after control of mainland Japan was returned to the Japanese government (Bugni, 1997). Immediately after the war, the US military forcibly confiscated the land of thousands of locals to build a series of bases across the island; land which, as in the case of Guam, has largely not been returned (Bugni, 1997, Shorrock, 2005). Even after Okinawa was returned to the Japanese, US forces remained on the island (and on the mainland) under the "Treaty of Mutual Cooperation and Security" and the "Status of Forces Agreement," signed by Japan and the US after the war (Bugni, 1997). Accordingly, as in the case of Guam, US military bases located on Okinawa have played important roles in the Korean, Vietnam, Iraq, and Afghanistan Wars (Inoue et al., 1998).

Currently, the US military maintains approximately 32 bases and facilities on Okinawa (Mitchell, 2017). Together, these facilities sprawl across nearly 20 percent of Okinawa's land; a number that becomes particularly staggering when considering that the island itself only comprises about 0.6 percent of Japan's total land area (Bugni, 1997). Important facilities include Kadena Air Base, which is the largest US Air Force base in Asia, and Marine Corps Air Station Futenma. Approximately 28,000 US soldiers, primarily from the Air Force and Marines are stationed on Okinawa (out of nearly 47,000 stationed across Japan) (Bugni, 1997).

Over the years, this presence has caused tension between local Okinawans and the US military, leading to significant protests. In particular, Okinawans have been angered that despite their island's tiny size relative to mainland Japan, Okinawa hosts over 50 percent of the US military's deployment to the country (Inoue et al., 1998). Other issues include the constant nuisance and often danger of military operations (and in particular aircraft), destabilization of the local economy (or the centering of the economy around providing services for US soldiers), and crimes committed by US soldiers, including rape and murder (Inoue et al., 1998). In an absolutely horrific example of such crime, three US Marines raped a 12-year-old girl in 1995 (Denyer and Kashiwagi, 2018). This event led to widespread outrage among locals and (increased) calls for the US military to leave the island altogether (Inoue et al., 1998). In response, the Japanese and US governments initially promised to close Marine Corps Air Station Futenma, but later decided to simply relocate the base up the coast to Nago City, in Henoko Bay, causing fresh outrage (Inoue et al., 1998, WP, 2018). With construction of the new base just underway, around 70,000 Okinawan residents held a protest against the relocation in August 2018 ("Tens of thousands rally for removal of US base from Japanese island," 2018).

Again similar to the situation in Guam, pollution from US military facilities and bases is another serious issue in Okinawa. Much of this pollution/contamination can be traced back to two main bases; Kadena Air Base, and MCAS Futenma, both of which are located in densely populated areas (especially MCAS Futenma), as well as other US Marines facilities, including Camp Hansen and Camp Schwab. According to documents obtained through the Freedom of Information Act (FOIA) by the investigative journalist Jon Mitchell, a large number of spills and incidents involving hazardous and toxic materials have contaminated the soil and waters on and around Kadena Air Base over the years (Mitchell, 2016). Such hazardous materials reportedly include arsenic, lead, PCBs, asbestos, and dioxin (Mitchell, 2016). Furthermore, from the years 1998 to 2015, 415 "environmental incidents" occurred, spilling 40,000 liters of jet fuel, 13,000 liters, and around 480,000 liters of sewage onto lands and waterways in and around the base (Mitchell, 2016). Furthermore, from 2001 to 2015, 23,000 liters of fire-fighting foam (which often contains PFAS chemicals) were spilled, contaminating water around the base (Mitchell, 2016). In recent years, evidence has come to light suggesting that various PFAS chemicals, including PFOA and PFOS, can cause cancer, as well as developmental, immunological, and reproductive problems ("Basic Information of PFAS," EPA, 2018). Over the years, US servicemembers stationed at Kadena Air Base have reported a number of severe illnesses, including cancer, autoimmune, respiratory, and neurological problems in themselves, and in their children (Mitchell, 2016). Not only have local Okinawans been impacted by the pollution then; US servicemembers have been harmed as well.

In addition to Kadena Air Base, MCAS Futenma has been a large source of environmental contamination on Okinawa over the years as well. Again according to the research of journalist Jon Mitchell, the land and water surrounding three US Marines bases (MCAS Futenma, Camp Hansen, and Camp Schwab) have been polluted by 270 separate spills of fuels, antifreeze, and water/POL (Petroleum, Oils, and Lubricants) mixtures. MCAS Futenma has taken the brunt of these incidents, with 14,003 liters of fuel spilled from 2005-2016 (Mitchell, 2017). In addition to fuel spills, elevated levels of both PFOA and PFOS have been found in groundwater downstream of Futenma, probably stemming from the use of PFAS-containing firefighting foams ("Banned chemicals contaminate groundwater near US bases on Okinawa," 2017). And in 1981, 100 barrels, some probably containing Agent Orange, were discovered buried next to a runway after elevated levels of chemicals were discovered in runoff from the base ("Agent Orange's deadly legacy spreads to Japan," 2012).

Given the environmental, cultural, social, and political impacts of US military bases described above in Guam and Okinawa, it is clear that the military's presence represents a new form of colonialism in both locations. This new form of colonialism, which can be theorized as military base colonialism, is distinct from both traditional colonialism and neocolonialism. In general, traditional colonialism involves the direct political, economic, and social control of one nation over that of another nation and/or territory (Wickens and Sandlin, 2007). In essence, traditional colonialism implies complete subjugation of the people and lands of one entity by that of another (Wijesinghe, 2017). In contrast, neocolonialism can be seen as a subtler form of control, allowing one group to exploit and dominate the other through the mechanisms of the global market (i.e. capitalism) (Condit and Kavoori, 1998). Military base colonialism, on the other hand, can be seen as the domination of a nation (or part of nation, in the case of Okinawa) or territory through the establishment of military bases on that nation or territory's land. This domination does not take the form of direct political control, but instead negatively impacts and influences the culture, society, economy, environment, and public health of people living adjacent to military bases and facilities.

In both Guam and Okinawa then, the US military base presence can be seen as just such a form of military base colonialism. Accordingly, both locations have been impacted in a number of different ways. In terms of cultural issues, local residents on both Guam and Okinawa have been heavily impacted over the decades by the confiscation of their lands by the military. On the island of Guam, the US military currently controls around one third of the land, much of which used to belong to the indigenous Chamorro people (Owen, 2010, Babauta, 2018). This loss of land has negatively impacted traditional Chamorro farming practices, as well as limited access to sites containing artifacts (such as stone pillars, called latte stones, and pottery remnants) of cultural and historical significance to the Chamorro people (Babauta, 2018; Owen, 2010). In Okinawa, where military bases cover about 20 percent of the island's land, the situation is similar

(Bugni, 1997). The military's confiscation of land from thousands of farmers after WWII fundamentally changed the way Okinawans lived their lives as a mainly agricultural people, forcing a shift towards other livelihoods as described below ("Ryukyu Islands," Encyclopedia Britannica, 2018; Shorrock, 2005).

The US military presence has also had enormous social consequences for Guam and Okinawa. In both locations, the constant military presence has threatened communities with real physical danger. In Okinawa, the close proximities of US bases such as Kadena Air Base and MCAS Futenma to commercial areas, houses, and even schools put people in constant danger from mishaps involving aircraft and other accidents (Kawakami, 2018). Around-the-clock military operations can be a serious nuisance/annoyance to local populations as well (Inoue, 1998). In Guam, the presence of US bases has made the entire island into a potential North Korean missile target (Yuen, 2017). Another social issue stemming from the US base presence in both locations is crime. As mentioned above, crimes committed by US soldiers in Okinawa in particular have included rape and murder (Inoue, 1998).

The US military presence in Guam and Okinawa has significantly altered and subsequently reshaped the local economies in both locations as well. In Guam, the arrival of the US military caused the economy to shift from mainly subsistence agriculture to cash and wage-based labor (Owen, 2010). In Okinawa, a similar shift led to the establishment of a largely service-based economy that provided for US soldiers, including the establishment of various bars, restaurants, and brothels, especially in the years immediately after WWII (Inoue, 1998). Finally, although such economic shifts may seem negative (especially with regards to an increase in prostitution), it has been argued by some that the US presence in both locations has in fact benefitted local economies, through the creation of jobs and spending by US servicemembers and their families (Kawakami, 2018). Others would argue that these benefits have been outweighed by the negative impacts of the military's presence, including a loss of access to land, increased crime, environmental contamination, and the danger and nuisance of military operations.

Additionally, local politics in both Guam and Okinawa have been dominated by the presence of the US military. In Okinawa, a major issue in local elections has been the planned relocation of MCAS Futenma to Nago City in Henoko Bay, as well as the US military presence and its impacts as described above (Kawakami, 2018, Denyer and Kashiwagi, 2018). In Guam however, the situation is further complicated by the fact that the island is a sovereign territory of the US, and that, although its inhabitants are US citizens, they cannot vote in US national elections or send voting representatives to Congress (Burrows, 2017; "Guam Territory Profile," 2018). Given these facts, it is unsurprising that many argue Guam is still a traditional colonial possession of the US (Babauta, 2018). As a consequence, local political debate on the island is not only dominated by the issue of the US military presence, but by questions of sovereignty as well (Yuen, 2017).

Military base colonialism in both Guam and Okinawa was only made possible through the territorialization and therefore control of land by the US government, however. Without this process of territorialization, the myriad impacts of US military base colonialism described above would not be felt by local populations in Guam and Okinawa today. As theorized by Nancy Lee Peluso and Christian Lund in their literature review "New Frontiers of Land Control: Introduction," territorialization is a form of land control carried out primarily by State actors (Peluso and Lund, 2011). As such, territorialization involves the claiming of land by the government for a specific use, such as industrial agriculture, forestry, or conservation (Peluso and Lund, 2011). Crucially, the exclusion and even displacement of people from land often occurs as a result of territorialization (Peluso and Lund, 2011).

In Guam and Okinawa then, the current US military presence was established through the territorialization of land. As mentioned above, around one third or more of Guam's land and approximately 20 percent or more of Okinawa's land was claimed by the US government after WWII (Babauta, 2018; Bugni, 1997). The only significant difference between this claiming of land by the US government and the broader process of territorialization as described by Peluso and Lund lies in the intended use of the land. Rather than territorializing land for use in agriculture, industry, or even conservation, the US government claimed land on Guam and Okinawa for the express purpose of constructing military bases and other facilities. In both locations, this territorialization led to the exclusion and displacement of locals from the land they had owned for generations, or even thousands of years. In Guam, the indigenous Chamorro people lost large portions of their ancestral lands, while in Okinawa, thousands of farmers lost their lands (Babauta, 2018; Shorrock, 2005). Seemingly without thought to the wishes of those living on both islands, the US military established a presence in the Asia-Pacific through the territorialization of land on Guam and Okinawa, leading to the current status-quo.

Finally, this claiming of land by the US government, and the subsequent military base colonialism that it established, has led to environmental discrimination by the US military in both Guam and Okinawa. Generally speaking, environmental discrimination can be defined as discrimination in the establishment, interpretation and enforcement of environmental regulations based on race, ethnicity, gender, culture, or socioeconomic status (Professor Adunbi). More broadly, environmental discrimination can also be theorized under the framework of distributive justice, as discussed by John Rawls and others, in which justice is defined in part as the equal distribution of both goods and ills throughout society (Schlosberg, 2007). In this framework, environmental discrimination and more broadly environmental injustice can be defined as the disproportionate distribution of environmental hazards based on race, ethnicity, gender, culture, or socioeconomic status.

In light of these definitions, the US military's choice to locate bases in Guam and Okinawa constitutes environmental discrimination, based on the race/ethnicity and socioeconomic status of the people living in both locations. In both Guam and Okinawa, local populations differ significantly in terms of race/ethnicity from the mainland US and mainland Japan, respectively. As mentioned above, the indigenous Chamorro people make up nearly 40 percent of the population in Guam, while Filipinos and other peoples of Asian descent make up large parts of the population as well (Burrows, 2017). Additionally, poverty is significantly higher in Guam than in the United States proper. According to the CIA Factbook, 23 percent of Guam's population lives under the poverty line, compared to 15.1 percent in the US ("CIA Factbook, Population Below Poverty Line," 2018). According to another source, about one in four households on the island has a yearly income of less than $3,000 to $20,000 (Dumat-ol Dalemo, 2015).

Similarly, the people of Okinawa are of a slightly different ethnicity than mainland Japanese, due to their unique heritage as a part of the former Kingdom of Ryukyu (Denyer and Kashiwagi, 2018; "Ryukyu Islands," Encyclopedia Britannica, 2018). In addition, Okinawa Prefecture (which includes the island of Okinawa) is the poorest prefecture in Japan (Inoue et al., 1998). Based on these facts then, contamination from US military bases on both islands amounts to environmental discrimination, whether intentional or not. In both cases, it seems likely that the minority and low-income status of each population (in comparison to the mainland US and Japan) has made the military's continued use of land on both islands significantly easier. In no small part because of their marginalized status, the protests and complaints of the people of Guam and Okinawa have been ignored at the expense of US military hegemony in the Asia-Pacific region.

In conclusion, the US military's occupation of bases throughout the Asia-Pacific and in particular in Guam and Okinawa represents a new form of colonialism. This military base colonialism is characterized not by outright domination but rather a subtler form of control, designed primarily to influence the region as a whole rather than those places actually hosting bases and facilities. Crucially, this military base colonialism has only been made possible through a territorializing process of land control, carried out by the US government in the years immediately after WWII. Finally, this new colonialism and control of land has allowed the US military to contaminate and pollute the environments and communities immediately surrounding its bases, largely without consequence. Whether intentional or not, the release of this contamination constitutes environmental discrimination, given its disproportionate impact on various low-income and racially, ethnically, and culturally diverse groups, such as the indigenous Chamorro on Guam and native Okinawans on Okinawa. In sum, despite the US military's intention to provide security and stability to the Asia-Pacific region, its presence has had significant consequences for those living next to its bases, in terms of the environment but also in terms of a wide range of political, cultural, social and economic issues. As a whole then, the US military presence in the Asia-Pacific, as well as throughout the rest of the world, bears a closer investigation by academia. Just because the US military is one the most powerful militaries in the world does not mean that its actions should go unquestioned.

References

About United States Indo-Pacific Command. (2018). *US Military*. http://www.pacom.mil/About-USINDOPACOM/

About USFJ. (2018). *US Military*. http://www.usfj.mil/About-USFJ/

Agent Orange's deadly legacy spreads to Japan. (2012). *RT*. https://www.rt.com/news/agent-orange-buried-okinawa-932/

ANDERSEN AIR FORCE BASE Site Profile (2018). *EPA*. https://cumulis.epa.gov/supercpad/CurSites/srchsites.cfm

Banned chemicals contaminate groundwater near US bases on Okinawa. (2017). *RT*. https://www.rt.com/usa/385233-okinawa-pfos-water-contamination/

Basic Information on PFAS (2016). *EPA*. https://www.epa.gov/pfas/basic-information-pfas

Borja, J.I. (2017). 25 years later, Andersen Air Force Base still cleaning up contamination, EPA says. *Pacific Daily News*. https://www.guampdn.com/story/news/2017/10/15/25-years-later-andersen-air-force-base-still-cleaning-up-contamination-epa-says/764211001/

Burrows, I. (2017). Where is Guam and how many US troops are there? *ABC*. https://www.abc.net.au/news/2017-08-09/where-is-guam-and-how-many-us-troops-are-there/8788566

Bugni, T. M. (1997). The Continued Invasion: Assessing the United States Military Presence on Okinawa through 1996 Notes. *Suffolk Transnational Law Review, 21*, 85-112. https://heinonline.org/HOL/P?h=hein.journals/sujtnlr21&i=93

Condit, C. M., and Kavoori, A. P. (1998). Postcolonial or neocolonial? Defining the grounds of research in global communication studies: Getting past the latest "post": Assessing the term "post-colonial." *Critical Studies in Mass Communication*, 15(2), 195-203. https://doi.org/10.1080/15295039809367042

Copp, T. (2018). DoD: At least 126 bases report water contaminants linked to cancer, birth defects. *Military Times*. https://www.militarytimes.com/news/your-military/2018/04/26/dod-126-bases-report-water-contaminants-harmful-to-infant-development-tied-to-cancers/

De Castro, R. (1994). U.S. Grand Strategy in Post-Cold War Asia-Pacific. *Contemporary Southeast Asia*, 16(3), 342–353. https://www.jstor.org/stable/25798254

Denyer, S., and Kashiwagi, A. (2018). In Japan's Okinawa island, U.S. military bases take center stage in election. https://www.washingtonpost.com/world/asia_pacific/in-japans-okinawa-island-us-military-bases-take-center-stage-in-election/2018/09/28/984fc0bc-c1b7-11e8-9451-e878f96be19b_story.html

Dumat-ol Daleno, G. (2015). Spotlight on poverty. *Pacific Daily News*. https://www.guampdn.com/story/news/2015/07/26/spotlight-poverty/30607525/

Fluorinated Chemicals Taint Water at Scores of Military Bases, Neighboring Communities: DOD Discloses Locations for First Time. (2018). *EcoWatch*. https://www.ecowatch.com/water-military-bases-chemicals-2566989573.html

Guam profile. (2018). *BBC News*. https://www.bbc.com/news/world-asia-16517384

Holmes, O. (2017). What is the US military's presence near North Korea? *The Guardian*. https://www.theguardian.com/us-news/2017/aug/09/what-is-the-us-militarys-presence-in-south-east-asia

Inoue, M. S., Purves, J., and Selden, M. (1998). Okinawa Citizens, US Bases, and the Security of Asia. *Economic and Political Weekly, 33*(6), 264-266. http://www.jstor.org/stable/4406373

Kawakami, T. (2018). The Contentious U.S. Presence in Okinawa, Japan. *World Policy.* https://worldpolicy.org/2018/04/05/the-contentious-us-presence-in-okinawa-japan/

Lawrence, M. J., Stemberger, H. L. J., Zolderdo, A. J., Struthers, D. P., and Cooke, S. J. (2015). The effects of modern war and military activities on biodiversity and the environment. *Environmental Reviews*, 23(4), 443-460. https://doi.org/10.1139/er-2015-0039

Letman, J. (2016). Proposed US military buildup on Guam angers locals who liken it to colonization. *The Guardian.* https://www.theguardian.com/us-news/2016/aug/01/guam-us-military-marines-deployment

Limtiaco, S. (2017). Guam's strategic importance: From coaling station to tip of the spear. *Pacific Daily News.* https://www.guampdn.com/story/news/2018/09/02/guams-strategic-importance-coaling-station-tip-spear/1048589002/

Lutz, C. (2018). Bureaucratic Weaponry and the Production of Ignorance in Military Operations on Guam. *Current Anthropology.* https://doi.org/10.1086/699937

Mitchell, J. (2016). Contamination at Largest US Air Force Base in Asia: Kadena, Okinawa. *The Asia-Pacific Journal: Japan Focus.* https://apjjf.org/2016/09/Mitchell.html

Mitchell, J. (2017). Environmental Contamination at US Marine Corps Bases on Okinawa. *Civilian Exposure.* https://www.civilianexposure.org/environmental-contamination-at-us-marine-corps-bases-on-okinawa/

Owen, A. (2010). Guam culture, immigration and the US military build-up. *Asia Pacific Viewpoint, 51*(3), 304-318. https://doi.org/10.1111/j.1467-8373.2010.01433.x

Peluso, N. L., and Lund, C. (2011). New frontiers of land control: Introduction. *Journal of Peasant Studies, 38*(4), 667-681. https://doi.org/10.1080/03066150.2011.607692

Population Below Poverty Line. (2018). *The World Factbook, Central Intelligence Agency.* https://www.cia.gov/library/publications/the-world-factbook/fields/2046.html

Ryukyu Islands: archipelago, Japan. (2018). *Encyclopedia Britannica.* https://www.britannica.com/place/Ryukyu-Islands

Seaton, P. (2017). Japanese Empire in Hokkaido. *Oxford Research Encyclopedia of Asian History.* https://doi.org/10.1093/acrefore/9780190277727.013.76

Shorrock, T. (2005). Okinawa and the U.S. Military in Northeast Asia. *Institute for Policy Studies.* https://ips-dc.org/okinawa_and_the_us_military_in_northeast_asia/

Tens of thousands rally for removal of US base from Japanese island. (2018). *CNBC.* https://www.cnbc.com/2018/08/12/tens-of-thousands-rally-for-removal-of-us-base-from-japanese-island.html

The US has a massive military presence in the Asia-Pacific. Here's what you need to know about it. (2017). *PRI.* https://www.pri.org/stories/2017-08-11/us-has-massive-military-presence-asia-pacific-heres-what-you-need-know-about-it

Toxic bases in the Pacific. (2005). *Nautilus Institute for Security and Sustainability.* https://nautilus.org/apsnet/toxic-bases-in-the-pacific/

Vine, D. (2017). List of U.S. Military Bases Abroad, 2017. *AU Digital Research Archive.* https://dra.american.edu/islandora/object/auislandora%3A55685

Vine, D. (2015). Where in the World Is the U.S. Military? *Politico Magazine.* https://www.politico.com/magazine/story/2015/06/us-military-bases-around-the-world-119321.html

Webb, W. (2017). U.S. Military Is World's Biggest Polluter. (2017). *EcoWatch.* https://www.ecowatch.com/military-largest-polluter-2408760609.html

Wickens, C. M., and Sandlin, J. A. (2007). Literacy for What? Literacy for Whom? The Politics of Literacy Education and Neocolonialism in UNESCO- and World Bank-Sponsored Literacy Programs. *Adult Education Quarterly, 57*(4), 275-292. https://doi.org/10.1177/0741713607302364

Wijesinghe, S. N. R., Mura, P., and Bouchon, F. (2017). Tourism knowledge and neocolonialism - a systematic critical review of the literature. *Current Issues in Tourism*, 1-17. https://doi.org/10.1080/13683500.2017.1402871

Woody, C, and Cheng, J. (2018). Here's the hardware the world's top 25 militaries have in their arsenals. *Business Insider.* https://www.businessinsider.com/here-are-the-worlds-most-powerful-militaries-2018-2

Yuen, S. (2017). Threatened for being a military island, many in Guam don't even want to be part of the US. *CNBC.* https://www.cnbc.com/2017/08/18/threatened-for-being-a-military-island-many-in-guam-dont-even-want-to-be-part-of-the-us.html

Excellence in Upper-Level Writing (Humanities)

Tinker, Tailor, Author, Masochist:
The Ishiguro Novel as a Field Experiment in Pain
by Verity Sturm
*From English 398.002: Clones, Detectives, Artists, and a Shiny Nobel
Prize (The Case of Ishiguro)*
Nominated by Andrea Zemgulys

This is an essay that organizes and evaluates most of the oeuvre of a challenging contemporary writer, Kazuo Ishiguro. Sturm figured out a master figure to center her reading of his novels -- the wound -- and it really works to address his novels in both style and content. Notably, she takes on his most difficult novel -- The Unconsoled -- to ground her ideas, as well as our more challenging secondary sources. In other words, I hope it is evident to the committee that her style is excellent, but I also wish to point out that its content and range is ambitious. I remarked to Sturm: "This essay was a thrill to read. The use of the wound as a master figure for reading the works of Ishiguro is compelling, thoughtful, and wonderfully argued; the essay admirably develops its own trope of the constellation. I was with you every step of the way, curious and compelled. And I learned a great deal from the essay: I never myself felt like I'd gotten a grip on Brodsky's [of The Unconsoled] pain, and now I feel confidently educated about it."

Andrea Zemgulys

Tinker, Tailor, Author, Masochist: The Ishiguro Novel as a Field Experiment in Pain

To put it bluntly, Kazuo Ishiguro isn't particularly fun to read. His characters suffer, and their suffering, whether by direct cause or symbolic energy, tends to determine the fate of their novel-worlds. When figuring Ishiguro's individual works into a macroscopic constellation, however, the manner by which their suffering is expressed appears to evolve. As Ishiguro ages and transforms as a novelist, so does his literary depiction of pain. Ishiguro's first few novels present pain as a psychological plot device; however, as his writing matures into different genres and narrative voices, pain seems to accordingly crystallize into a more corporeal motif. This migration of portrayal from the internal and narrative to the external and stylistic, in effect, works to make the pains of his novels more obvious and accessible. Furthermore, the evolution of pain throughout Ishiguro's works necessitates a responding evolution in how his characters both acknowledge and treat such pain. Ishiguro's novels accordingly seem to explore the comparative impact and efficacy of varying forms and relationships of pain—an ongoing, ever-evolving experiment in how pain may be best expressed, managed, and, ultimately, felt.

Pain first surfaces as a tangible theme about halfway through Ishiguro's writing career in his notably bizarre fever dream of a novel *The Unconsoled* (1995). Although most all of Ishiguro's novels imply suffering to some capacity, *The Unconsoled* is the first to specifically present pain as a dominating theme, offering a sturdy scaffold for discourse on the topic through the motif of the wound, first introduced by the recovering alcoholic Leo Brodsky about halfway through the novel. While attempting to stage a reunion with his ex-lover, a realm of particular anguish for the volatile conductor, Brodsky expresses that he suffers from "a pain… [not] an emotional pain… [but] a wound [he] got many years ago [that has] always given [him] trouble… Bad pain" (*Unconsoled* 308). When again queried whether he's "referring to a wound of the heart," Brodsky reiterates that he's "[not] being poetic" and "meant simply, [he] had a wound" from a past injury in Russia that "never healed properly" and thus motivated much of his drinking (*Unconsoled* 308). Brodsky's insistence on the physical nature of his pain is especially remarkable given the overtly emotional context of the scene—in effect, the decision to stage the literary inauguration of "the wound" during a scene of considerable emotional tension inevitably associates the psychological with the physical. Consequently, in terms of interpretation, there is certainly a case to read Brodsky's old Russian wound as a representation of his more internal, emotional turmoil, despite (or perhaps due to) his staunch denial of exactly that.

After establishing the unexpectedly physical nature of his wound, Brodsky launches into an extended, reflective musing on pain management, preaching that "these old wounds... they stay the same for years. You think you've got the measure of it. Then you get old and they start to grow again." (*Unconsoled* 309). Brodsky continues to prattle on about his wound in a manner that grows increasingly theoretical, eventually remarking that, despite the animosity with which he seems to generally speak of his injury, his wound "fascinates" him, and the act of "caressing" the wound grants him a sort of consolation akin to the music he conducts for a living (*Unconsoled* 313). Thus, although Brodsky's wound afflicts him with bitterly chronic pain, a sort of "fascinating" mutual relationship persists between the pain and the pained. This relationship, and its curiously positive attributes, is one of the most strikingly cogent, traceable themes of the novel.

The verb "caress" appears almost as frequently as "wound" in the novel, arguably a motif of its own. Brodsky appears to consider the act of "caressing" to be a sort of solidarity-making with his wound: although the wound's appearance may change with time, when "you touch it... you know it's the same, your old friend" (*Unconsoled* 313). The oddly fond, friendly relationship Brodsky cultivates with his wound (seemingly represented by the tender verb "caress") must be advantageous to some degree, as he actively advises others to employ such a mechanism of pain management in their respective sufferings, a sort of unrequited counseling evident in a scene where he crashes a funeral (uninvited) to do precisely that:

> Then Brodsky said tenderly:
> "Someone you love has died. This is a precious moment."
> I felt the ends of his raincoat brush the back of my head, and I realised he was extending a hand down towards the widow.
> "This is a precious time. Come. Caress your wound now. It will be there for the rest of your life. But caress it now, while it's raw and bleeding. Come." (*Unconsoled* 372)

Brodsky's repetition of the imperative "come" imbues his advice with a sense of urgency, explicated in his insistence to pay the wound attention "while it's raw and bleeding," as if the most opportune time to provoke the wound is when it is most vulnerable. The denotation of the imperative "come" also emphasizes the ethos of solidarity wrapped up in "caressing" the wound by way of its inclusive tone. In a sense, Brodsky appears to be inviting the widow to know her wound *alongside* him, implying a sense of solidarity between Brodsky and the widow through their shared, chosen responsibility to caress their wounds. In addition to "come," the repetition of the adjective "precious" in this scene associates the process of "caressing" the wound with considerable wonder and necessity, adding to the persuasive power of Brodsky's approach. According to Brodsky, the process of deliberately feeling the wound at the peak of its pain is a sacred experience capable of bringing the individual closer to their pain, and the pained individuals closer to each other.

The repeated motifs of "the wound" and "caressing" throughout *The Unconsoled* appear especially notable due to their contextual clarity—when situated in the jarring, rule-bending bedlam of this particular novel, the explicit repetition of these terms offers an ironic sense of stability to the confused narrative. Thus, the imperative to caress the wound appears as one of the most concrete takeaways from *The Unconsoled*—a tenet so randomly stable in comparison to the rest of its novel-host that it seems like it must belong to a larger framework. When considering Ishiguro's works macroscopically, this could very well be the case. His novels following *The Unconsoled* all seem to interact with the impact of choosing to acknowledge pain—the benefits, the consequences, what happens when the choice is impossible, and what happens when the choice is manipulated. Despite its infamy (or perhaps due to!), *The Unconsoled* seems to present a free agent of a theme that reverberates throughout Ishiguro's entire career, providing the common ground necessary to conceptualize the *body* of Ishiguro's work beyond a novel-by-novel analysis. With "the wound" as an appropriately macabre polaris, Ishiguro's novels may be collectively figured into an extended commentary on pain theory.

Ishiguro's 2005 dystopia *Never Let Me Go* further explores the pain management potential of "caressing" by experimenting with a world in which such an option isn't so readily available. *The Unconsoled* habitually emphasizes the importance of the individual to "caress" their own wound, infusing the process with a sense of willful choice. In contrast, the ambiguously oppressive society of *Never Let Me Go* effectively strips individuals from this agency by seizing the means of the entire "pain-ing" process. Indeed, pain operates differently in *Never Let Me Go* than it does the rest of Ishiguro's novels—the planned, systematic, and overtly lethal harvesting of organs that the novel's authority imposes upon its minorities renders pain a tool of the state rather than an experience of the individual. Furthermore, the manner in which the state "pains" its oppressed isn't designed to leave room for "caressing" of any sort. Since the state's use of pain is in the interest of subduing an entire demographic, it is exhaustive and debilitating in nature—regular, compounding organ excisions render "donors" totally (and successfully) helpless in terms of pain management and recovery. Kathy H. recognizes this utter, intentional helplessness in her good friend Ruth whom, after a series of donations, appears "like she was willing her eyes to see right inside herself, so she could control and marshal all the better the separate areas of pain in her body" (*NLMG* 236). Ruth is unnaturally afflicted with so many intense pains that she struggles to remain lucid in their wake—"still conscious, but [not] accessible… [seized by] flood[s] of pain that ma[k]e her twist away" (*NLMG* 236). While Brodsky and the widow grapple with the daunting decision to embrace and engage with their wounds, Ruth is so disadvantaged that she struggles to simply survive and, in fact, dies before recovering enough to wrestle with any sort of pain management strategies.

When comparing *The Unconsoled* with *Never Let Me Go*, the ability to personally acknowledge and engage with one's own pain appears to possess considerable power—enough to mobilize a shockingly cruel autocracy. Although not explicitly addressed, the question of whether the "donors" of *Never Let Me Go* could manage a rebellion lingers on the margins of the novel, shrouded in its depressingly intuitive answer: a legion of bedridden, organ-depleted cripples is hardly a legion. When read in the spirit of *The Unconsoled* and caressing, this grim conclusion is substantiated: what spirit would motivate such a rebellion if the members afflicted are incapable of postulating and coming to terms with the unjust reality of their wounds? Brodsky manages to assume something along the lines of this rebel flair, demonstrated by his enthusiastic empowerment of the widow; in contrast, Ruth can barely stay awake. Thus, the dystopian cruelty of *Never Let Me Go* seems related to disconnecting the individual from authority over their own physical pain. In fact, this subtle, effective manipulation of pain authority is illustrated earlier in the novel when a young Tommy suffers the crippling, embarrassing grip of paranoia (and its subsequent ridicules) when his classmates convince him that a superficial elbow wound, if not monitored impractically, renders him prone to "unzipping" the skin of his entire arm (*NLMG* 85). This seemingly innocuous interaction foreshadows a dynamic far more expansive in scope: one is at the mercy of whoever determines the way they experience their pain, be it their friends, their government, or themselves.

While *Never Let Me Go* presents a society in control of the way its subjects experience physical pain, Ishiguro's latest novel *The Buried Giant* (2015) seems to explore what would happen if such manipulation were psychological in nature. This feat is accomplished through setting: the post-Arthurian Britain of *The Buried Giant* is wrapped in an amnesic mist that prevents its subjects from accessing long-term memories. This mystical natural phenomena is later revealed to be of more sinister origins: following his defeat of the Saxons, King Arthur ordered for a preservation of the mist so that his new subjects forget about the violent slaughter of their people, essentially imposing docile obedience upon his kingdom by erasing whatever memories would painful enough to incite rebellion or unrest among them. This sort of political manipulation strikes a chord with *Never Let Me Go*: in both cases, the state insidiously seizes control over its subject's ability to manage their pain and, thus, induces submission, in one way or another. In this vein of thought, Ishiguro's later novels, perhaps, explicate the urgency with which Brodsky encourages the "caressing" of the wound—the ability to do so seems integral in terms of maintaining autonomy in potentially sinister situations.

Although Saxons and Britons alike in the *The Buried Giant* lose agency over their psychological pains, their physical pains remain very real, and tend to proliferate. In fact, one of the novel's elderly protagonists, Beatrice, demonstrates a remarkable Brodsky-esque intention to embrace her physical pains. Throughout *The Buried Giant*, Beatrice appears to be "nursing some secret pain… just below her ribcage" which is addressed and discussed often but, curiously, never complained about or treated (*BG* 46, 48). In fact, Beatrice spends much of the novel deflecting attention from her pain, regularly brushing it aside as "nothing but what's to be expected from the years," something undeserving of the worry or concern it seems to naturally accrue (*BG* 61). Beatrice's insistence on walking across the rugged, undeveloped, threateningly bewitched landscape of medieval Britain despite her age and pain exhibits a spirit of voluntary masochism—a staunch intention to *feel the thing*, no treatment needed, despite whatever inconvenience or negative affect it may entail. In the scope of the entire novel, Beatrice's *physical* pain seems a manifestation of her determination to acknowledge and accept the *psychological* pain of her memories, currently rendered unavailable by way of an enchanted, amnesic mist. When expressing enthusiasm to free herself of the mist, Beatrice is reminded that unpleasant memories lurk with the precious, to which she replies "[Axl and I will] have the bad ones come back too, even if they make us weep or shake with anger. For isn't it the life we've shared?" (*BG* 157). Beatrice appears adamant about embracing whatever beasts and pains may stir in her past, insisting that "Axl and [she] would remember [their] life together, whatever its shape, for it's been a dear thing to [them]... what's to fear?" (*BG* 157). Beatrice's insistence on caressing her pains traverses the line between physical and psychological, bringing her closer to the truth of her body, in terms of age and injury, and the truth of her past, exemplified by memory—the type of powerful solidarity-making with oneself, all the good and all the bad, that Brodsky so avidly encourages.

The Buried Giant seems to be the veritable magnum opus of pain management in its experimentation with intersecting vectors of pain-types: physical and psychological, individual and state-regulated. Ishiguro's latest novel seems to combine all the different aspects of pain and pain management he touches upon throughout his career. Interestingly enough, one of the most remarkable characters across Ishiguro's works emerges at the focus of this convergence: Edwin. From a young age, Edwin is made to suffer from the complicated physical and psychological ramifications of a wound that seems to bother those around him more than it does himself. Edwin himself describes the wound as "superficial—not as bad as many he had had before. And yet, because people believed it to be an ogre's bite, it [causes] all this trouble" (*BG* 91). Edwin is socially ostracized due to the fear his wound stokes in other people, and constantly advised by his few companions to physically attend to and mentally consider himself in terms of his wound so that he may survive, biologically and socially—a directive summarized in the appropriately ambiguous and vast scope of Father Jonus' conclusion "I believe it will heal if he takes good care of it" (*BG* 153). In a more metaphorical reading, Edwin realizes in his youth, far earlier than most of Ishiguro's major characters, that his wounds will come to define him, even though "there was no shame in how he faced his [initial, wound-giving] ordeal" (*BG* 92).

Edwin's predetermined fate is one of the most depressing elements of the novel, especially considering the boy's age and background (an absent mother, either dead or having deserted him). It is worthy of mention, however, that Edwin seems to be the closest thing to a hero discernible in Ishiguro's works.

Ishiguro's novels are notably near-devoid of heroics; in fact, his protagonists typically exude some combination of overtly unreliable, shockingly selfish, and paralyzingly timid. Consequently, the quintessential Ishiguro novel rarely ends on a note of resolution—including, honestly, *The Buried Giant*. But although *The Buried Giant* lacks most qualities definitive of the hero, it presents something related, and something entirely new to the Ishiguro novel: a warrior. Indeed, despite his depressing background and disadvantageous wound, the novel's third-person-omniscient voice directly states that "it was Edwin, not any of them, who possessed a warrior's soul" (*BG* 85). And although the term "warrior" is thrown about the novel in reference to a variety of men, it is only Edwin that is repeatedly singled out as possessing "a true warrior's spirit given only to a few," imbuing the boy with a more metaphysical significance than the rest (*BG* 298). Correlation is nowhere near scratching the surface of causation, but it's worthy of note that the one character across the vast majority of Ishiguro's career that even comes close to a hero is the boy who is forced at a young age to resign himself to his wound.

The evolution of pain and its relationships with agency and heroism throughout Ishiguro's career is dramatically persistent enough to provoke curiosity regarding the author's half of the bargain. Perhaps the most compelling argument for the Ishiguro novel as field experiment in pain, the act of "caressing" the wound as an exercise of agency, and the resignation of oneself to their affliction as the harbinger of heroism lies within the experiences of the author himself. To his credit, Ishiguro makes it difficult—with his consistent black turtlenecks, wireless frames, and deadpan delivery, the author curates a notoriously aloof persona in most all public appearances. Occasionally, however, an exciting kernel of emotion manages to poke through the cracks of an interview or speech long enough to create such an opportunity. In a 1995 interview with Maya Jaggi regarding the release of *The Unconsoled*, Ishiguro admits that "In a way, [his] first three books[1] were each an attempt to hone down the material used in the previous one… three attempts to cover the same territory," resulting in The Remains of the Day (1989)

---

1 *A Pale View of Hills* (1982), *An Artist of the Floating World* (1986), and *The Remains of the Day* (1989)

as a sort of final product, with which Ishiguro expresses he "was both pleased and disappointed by" (*Wasafiri*). In a rare moment of vulnerability, Ishiguro elaborates that the three novel process of perfecting *The Remains of the Day* led to a "strange dovetailing" in which he questioned whether he was writing about "someone obsessed with controlling every aspect of his life… in a voice like this, because [he was] afraid of losing control in the writing process" (*Wasafiri*). Ishiguro describes this implied, unintentional identification with Stevens, the fatally flawed perfectionist-protagonist of *The Remains of the Day*, as an "uncomfortable realisation" regarding his openness and honesty as a writer, and was consequently inspired to "write about more messy areas" of himself by way of relaxing the fine-tuned formality that came to define his early works (*Wasafiri*). This mid-career crisis inspired Ishiguro's infamous break from technical form in *The Unconsoled*, motivated by "an instinct that this is where the interesting stuff lies" and the belief that "you shouldn't keep going over old ground but should be digging around where it's uncomfortable" (*Wasafiri*).

The ethos of "digging around where it's uncomfortable" that inspired Ishiguro's rogue trip through *The Unconsoled* runs strikingly parallel in logic to Brodsky's philosophy on "caressing" the wound. In fact, the respective terminology of the two are practically interchangeable—"dig around" the "wound," "caress" the "uncomfortable"—all in the interest of tapping into what Ishiguro dubs "the interesting stuff;" Brodsky, the "fascinating". In this vein of thought, Ishiguro-through-Brodsky seems to express the interesting as inextricable from the painful; in other words (as everything now seems to be), the fascinating may *only* be accessed and, furthermore, expressed by engagement with those wounds.

For Ishiguro, these wounds seem deeply personal. In his 2017 Nobel Lecture, Ishiguro articulates his journey as a writer in unusually generous detail, revealing that much of the "peculiar energy" that launched his career as a writer was, in fact, "an urgent act of preservation" regarding his painful experience of identity displacement as a Japanese Briton (Ishiguro). In his speech, Ishiguro shares the "richly detailed place called 'Japan'… from which [he] drew a certain sense of [his] identity and [his] confidence," he imaginatively constructed as a nationally displaced youth, a fictionalized version of the country made "vivid and personal" by the fact that Ishiguro never physically returned to his home in his childhood (Ishiguro). In his mid-twenties, Ishiguro came to the realization that "the Japan that existed in [his] head might have always been an emotional construct put together by a child out of memory, imagination and speculation… [and that] this Japan of [his]—this precious place he grew up with—was getting fainter and fainter" with the years (Ishiguro). Ishiguro cites "this feeling, that ['his'] Japan was unique and at the same time terribly fragile—something not open to verification from the outside" as the sure and singular factor "that drove [him] on to work in that small room in Norfolk,"—that small room being the place where Ishiguro spent months struggling through his first novel, months during which he discovered the "new and urgent intensity" with which he wrote about Japan, months he plainly identifies as "crucial for [him], insofar as without them [he'd] probably never have become a writer" (Ishiguro).

While Ishiguro's interview with Maya Jaggi identifies his voice within Brodsky's, his Nobel Lecture illuminates a ghost of the author operating through Edwin. Both boys, at a young age, come to terms with a painful loss of innocence—a difficult process of acceptance and engagement that, although not *perfect* or *heroic*, empowers the individual with the agency of a warrior, or a writer. Most importantly, this process is "not open to verification from the outside;" in other words, the individual must choose to "caress" their wounds, whether among the dragons and pixies of medieval Britain or in a small room in Norfolk. Curiously enough, conscious or not, Ishiguro's works at large reflect a sort of macroscopic iteration of this internal process: the struggle towards perfection in the neurotic, self-conscious narration of *An Artist of the Floating World* and *The Remains of the Day* leading to a moment of clarity that manifests in the caress of *The Unconsoled*, which in turn permits the experimentation and exploration of *Never Let Me Go* and *The Buried Giant* that, finally, produces some sort of hero in all the pain.

Works Cited

Ishiguro, Kazuo. *The Unconsoled*. Penguin, 1995.

Ishiguro, Kazuo. *Never Let Me Go*. Penguin, 2005.[2]

Ishiguro, Kazuo. *The Buried Giant*. Penguin, 2015.[3]

"Kazuo Ishiguro Talks to Maya Jaggi." *Wasafiri*, Autumn 1995, pp. 20-24.

Ishiguro, Kazuo. "My Twentieth Century Evening—and Other Small Breakthroughs." 7 December 2017, Nobel Lecture. Provided by Instructor.

---

2 Referenced parenthetically as *NLMG* in paper
3 Referenced parenthetically as *BG* in paper

Excellence in Upper-Level Writing (Humanities)

Bitchin' About the Kitchen:
An Intersectional Review of Gender, Race, and Class in the Restaurant Industry
by Kelly Wester
From English 407.002: Food and Culture
Nominated by Supriya Nair

Kelly Wester's essay addresses the hierarchy of the professional kitchen with acuity and vigor. Her perceptive insights are enhanced by the meticulous research she did to support her arguments. Initially, the essay focused on the current significance of the #MeToo movement in challenging the ascendancy of professional male chefs, but it underwent revision after peer and instructor feedback. Kelly expanded her approach to a more inclusive intersectional perspective on the multiple inequalities of the restaurant industry, situating its problems in the competitive professionalism and the celebrity status of male "chefs," who gained prestige and power not conferred on female and/or nonwhite "cooks." Her sense of the ways in which class, gender, and race operate in both linked and distinct ways to perpetuate the discrimination in professional kitchen culture adds complexity to customary debates about domesticity and reveals the porousness of the private and public spheres.

Supriya Nair

Bitchin' About the Kitchen:
An Intersectional Review of Gender, Race, and Class in the Restaurant Industry

Mario Batali, Charlie Hallowell, John Besh. Once considered household names, these three men have since been ousted by the #MeToo movement for their sexual misconduct in the kitchen. Significantly, something their accusers have in common is that they have remained largely anonymous, fearful of the personal and professional ramifications that come from being the one to stand up to patriarchy. Meanwhile, the *Equal Employment Opportunity Commission* has reported that the largest number of sexual harassment charges come from the restaurant industry, and researchers have been puzzled as to why these statistics seem to be so pervasive within this professional environment (qtd. in "The Glass Floor"). Although in the past women have either been silenced or ignored, the #MeToo era presents the opportunity for a radical shift to break with industry norms. A cultural examination proves why this feminist undertaking must, at its core, be intersectional– applicable not only to white, middle-to-upper class women, but anyone who finds themselves on the chopping block because of gender, race, or class.

Masculinity pervades the kitchen in a systemic manner: gender discrimination finds its roots in Auguste Escoffier's militant brigade system. This top-down professional structure has often been credited with shaping the kitchen's "male-dominated hierarchy" (Black). Which is understandable, considering the way it assigns power to various actors mirrors a socially traditional assignment of privilege. Breaking down the chain of command into its concrete labels, a *chef de cuisine* (often a male) is above the *garde manger* (often a female), who is above, at the very bottom, the *plangeur*, or dishwasher (often a person of color or migrant). Essentially, station determines status: not only among the upper level staff such as the head, executive, or sous chefs, but the *commis* and apprentices as well. Although the position seems second to the chef, *garde manger* is just the politically correct way of saying 'Salad Girl' (Druckman "Skirt Steak" Kindle Location 5764). Some may argue that to disrupt this pecking order would be to upset the very foundation or tradition upon which the kitchen is built upon. But for those who have decided to break away from the traditional brigade system, the results have been highly rewarding. In the 1970s, when Alice Waters' *Chez Panisse* eliminated titles and rotated its staff through the brigade system, it taught the staff a very important lesson: "The higher you climb, the farther you get from the details" (Druckman "Skirt Steak" Kindle Location 374). Alice Waters has since received five *James Beard Awards*, and has been cited by many female chefs as an inspiration– proof that women *can* make it in the industry, if they are only given the opportunity to advance.

Underscoring the importance of Waters' resistance, hierarchy is not only ideologically harmful, but can at times prove to be physically endangering as well. After interviewing a number of professional female chefs, Maura Judkis and Emily Heil at the *Washington Post* report that women view the kitchen's culture of harassment as an "outgrowth" of Escoffier's brigade system (Judkis & Heil). When violence and abuse are normalized, if not ritualized (hazing is still viewed as a rite of passage for entry-level chefs), many turn a blind eye to its sexual forms. *Harvest2Order's* Liz Vankin wrote that after culinary school, she observed sexual harassment becoming an "expedient form of abuse… It's easier to make a woman feel bad about herself by touching her than just yelling that you're not cutting your parsley right" (qtd. in Judkis & Heil). As previously stated, these depictions or experiences of physical violence are not unique in the culinary world, and they are not isolated to women either. According to the *Harvard Business Review*, "in the restaurant industry… as many as 90% of women and 70% of men reportedly experience some form of sexual harassment" (Johnson & Madera). For those who were not born with the privilege of being a white, upper-class male, power dynamics make informed consent virtually impossible. Victims feel pressured to submit for fear of job loss or physical violence. For many, consent was never even part of the equation, as reports of rape and assault were shown to be numerous in the studied primary sources. However, the *National Restaurant Association's* quantitative data shows that the restaurant industry has continued to hold a notoriously high turnover rate of 70%, so it follows that reports of misconduct are often treated as if they will go away in their own time ("Hospitality Employee Turnover Rate Edged Higher in 2016"). This is why #MeToo infiltrating the professional kitchen is so important. It gives a voice and a presence to these survivors, who then find solidarity among others and do not feel as though they will inevitably be driven out by abuse.

When complaints fall on deaf ears, disempowered individuals must develop their own means of survival; they are often forced to fight violence with more violence. Chef Ulzii Hoyle describes the ramifications faced by women who fight back when she was interviewed by *The Washington Post*. After elbowing a male colleague who grabbed her buttocks and poked her in the genitals, the manager fired Hoyle, claiming that she was "too big of a liability," and telling her that "it would be best for everybody if you just left…" (qtd. in Judkis & Heil). At Rick Moonen's *RM Seafood*, Vaiva Labukaite reported harassment to the restaurant's management "and the next thing you know, my shifts were going down from five days a week to two days a week" (qtd. in Judkis & Heil). Other women share similar horror stories of a workplace environment being turned into a fight for one's bodily integrity. Maya Rotman-Zaid stuck a fork in a man's leg after he tried to feel her up, Beth Aretsky punched a man in the testicles after he repeatedly smacked her breast with a palette knife (Druckman "Skirt Steak" Kindle Location 755). Nonviolence is hard to maintain when your coworkers become attackers. If a woman isn't fired for reporting harassment, she is simply ignored. One anonymous server reported that when a male busser held a lighter underneath her hair, the general manager reprimanded but did not dismiss him (qtd. in Judkis & Heil). It is clear that the upper-level administration is aware of what goes on behind kitchen doors, but has turned a blind eye for the sake of maintaining the patriarchal hierarchy which financially benefits them.

This culture of abuse crosses not only gender, but racial lines as well. Joe Brown, an African American chef at *Mélange Cafe* recalls "at his first job, being choked and called a racial epithet by the chef" (qtd. in Ruhlman). These experiences can scar individuals, and leave them feeling unsafe or unwelcome in their place of work. It raises a very important question regarding whether minority chefs simply leave the industry, or if they are physically driven (perhaps more accurately, beaten) out. Marcus Samuelsson details a similar experience in his memoir, *Yes Chef*, as he watched a Japanese commis get punched in the stomach. He explains, "This was the dark side of the French tradition. All of the chefs had come up through that same brutal [brigade] system, where only the upper echelons had any sense of job security" (Samuelsson 170-71). Job security is even more precarious for those in the industry who are foreign-born or depend on their position to maintain a Work Visa. Maria Vazquez at *Art's Wings and Things* was raped by restaurant owner Arthur Boone, but as a monolingual Mexican immigrant with six children to support she could not afford to leave (qtd. in Judkis & Heil). Vazquez's demographic represents a large number of kitchen employees. According to the *National Restaurant Association*: "More than 23 percent of individuals employed at restaurants are foreign-born, versus 19 percent for the overall economy" ("Demographic Trends Illustrate Importance of Foreign-Born Workers"). Behind kitchen doors, that means the threat of deportation can be used as leverage over employees who would otherwise report harassment and abuse. Recall the structure of the brigade de cuisine: while women are placed beneath men, people of color are pushed even lower. If the #MeToo movement has proved anything, it's that there is strength in numbers. Coalition building between marginalized groups could present a very real threat to the white patriarchy struggling to maintain its hold on the kitchen industry. It is important that white, privileged females recognize that they can use their newfound influence to enact a greater good across class and racial lines as well.

Sexual harassment and physical violence are just some of the many ways the kitchen maintains its 'boy's club' status. Turning to finances, there is an important psychological and economic aspect to the way the restaurant industry values labor. For example, until Escoffier instilled the brigade system in the kitchen, being a chef was hardly lucrative. Historically the 'chef' status held domestic, blue-collar, racialized connotations. As Deborah Harris, a sociologist at Texas State University, writes in *Taking the Heat*: "It has been quite the journey from the 'chef as servant' mentality to the idea of 'chefs as the new rock stars'" (Harris 18). The "journey" that Harris describes was dependent upon the exclusion of women and racial minorities. Men constantly fight to maintain hierarchal boundaries so they can distinguish their work's "elite" status. As Meghan McCarron claims, "Behind the history of all-male brigades is an effort to distance restaurant cooking from home cooking, the result of a phenomenon some sociologists call 'precarious masculinity'" (McCarron). Indeed, one must wonder what separates the cooking of a domestic housewife from that of an 'avant-garde,' trailblazing male chef. Even these terms are gendered in an exclusionary way: women are cooks, men are chefs (Druckman "Why Are There No Great Women Chefs?"). Linguistically, there is no female variant of the word "chef," although some have tried to gender the title through "cheffin." The prevalent view held by women in the industry is that the less they try and make themselves stand out, the better. The risk of violence or backlash, some feel, is simply not worth trying to de-gender the boy's club. In an interview with Nicole Aita, a professional chef in the ever-competitive New York City, she remarked that men were constantly preferred for the "hot line" to the point that female coworkers would only put initials on their resumes because often times, their gender could preclude them from even getting an interview (Aita).

The way in which a chef can be gendered but also racialized based on name alone shows the intersectionality in a struggle just to enter the kitchen in an important position. Manhattan chef Lance Whitney Knowling was once being interviewed over the phone for a position at an upscale New Jersey restaurant. The restauranteur didn't realize Knowling was African American and joked, "I'd like to have somebody like you… I couldn't have a black guy or a Latin guy back there, because it would make my customers uncomfortable" (qtd. in Ruhlman). Needless to say, Knowling did not take the job. Previous generations seem to be sadly familiar with this kind of treatment, as a chef's historically low status also meant the position was deigned lower-class, so it was commonly typified as a minority occupation. The American family's "cook" (more accurately, servant) was a black female who received paltry pay for what was seen as a "domestic" duty. This changed in the 1960s and 70s when the restaurant industry became popularized, and economically viable. White chefs moved in and pushed the black chefs out, or into the lower stove positions. By the time *Alinea's* Milton Guzman, who is African American, decided he wanted to become a chef, his parents considered it to be "a step backward" for the race: "I don't think cooking, when parents want their children to grow up and prosper, [is] something that comes to mind" he explains, because of racial stereotypes such as "the house Negro or Aunt Jemima" (qtd. in Ruhlman). Power structures operate in a way that make it seem as though everyone has an equal opportunity to rise through the ranks, but given historical considerations and labor devaluation, the equality *of* that opportunity varies considerably by race and gender. In the coming years, it is critical the industry overcomes its prejudices in order to continue to thrive. As Meg McCarron points out, chefs may present themselves as 'trailblazers,' but "in reality, they're the ones stuck in the past. If men, especially white men, cannot re-examine their ideas about whose cooking has worth, what trails can they hope to blaze?" (McCarron).

Staying in the industry can present a different set of challenges for each chef. Women in particular are faced with an impossible task if they choose to have children and maintain a career. On one hand, the industry is structured in such a way that the sheer physical endurance expected in the kitchen can often not be maintained by an expectant mother. However, not every female chef even desires to have children. Nicole Aita recalled one woman who was told there would be no point in training women to begin with because they "just quit to have babies" (Aita). Traditional domesticity would place a woman in her kitchen at home, where she would presumably be the home-maker and child-bearer while her husband works. A number of trailblazing chefs like Mary Sue Milliken have reassigned this domestic role to their husbands– depending on only one parent's salary to get by, or by "outsourcing" the child care to a nanny (Druckman "Skirt Steak" Kindle Location 2712). As Traci des Jardins states, "[Men] don't have to give anything up because society doesn't expect the same things of them… And that's where we hit that stumbling block in our careers, because we are the keeper of home, and the keeper of relationship, and the keeper of children, by virtue of our sex. That's the stumbling block in the restaurant business for women … That's why women drop out" (qtd. in Druckman "Skirt Steak" Kindle Location 2715). But when minorities are pushed into performing the even more menial jobs which provide lower pay, this arrangement becomes impossible. The aforementioned Maria Vazquez is a mother of six. Financial restraints can leave these women with no other option than to face abuse for the sake of their children.

Women should not feel as though they need to retreat to the East Coast's female food haven in order to feel safe or accepted in their craft (Valenti). Working together, there is real potential for women to excel and grow through mentorship and opportunity. And while female chefs like Giada De Laurentiis, Ree Drummond, and Ina Garten have a big media presence, researcher Kelsi Matwick has found that "discursive practices [here, cookbooks] can help produce and reproduce unequal power relations between (for instance) social classes, women and men, and ethnic/cultural majorities and minorities through the ways in which they represent things and position people" (Matwick 536). Furthermore, not everyone has the financial means to pack up and leave– family obligations and financial constraints often stand in the way of career relocation. But is it any wonder these individuals feel discouraged when the jury for *San Pellegrino's* 2018 Young Chef competition looks like it does in Figure 1?

AFRICA & MIDDLE
EAST JURY
ANNOUNCED FOR
S.PELLEGRINO
YOUNG CHEF 2018

THE S.PELLEGRINO
YOUNG CHEF JURY
FOR SPAIN AND
PORTUGAL IS READY

HERE IS THE LOCAL
CHEF JURY FOR
BENELUX

FOUR TOP CHEFS
NAMED IN JAPAN
LOCAL COMPETITION
JURY

FRANCE REVEALS
THEIR JURY FOR
S.PELLEGRINO
YOUNG CHEF LOCAL
COMPETITIONS 2017

MEET THE FIVE
FOOD EXPERTS
FORMING THE
LOCAL JURY
FOR

MEET THE TRIO OF
CHEFS WHO WILL
JUDGE THE LOCAL
FINAL IN SOUTH
AMERICA

MEET THE JURY FOR
SCANDINAVIA AND
BALTICS IN THE
S.PELLEGRINO
YOUNG CHEF LOCAL
FINALS

Figure 1: Photograph of San Pellegrino's 'Young Chef' Juries (Crenn)

Even if one has the resolve to tough it out, awards statistics show that recognition will be unlikely. Accolades are a manifestation of one's effort and accomplishments, a signal that your contribution to the culinary world is both acknowledged and respected. Nevertheless, when *Eater* compiled data and statistics of female representation in food, women accounted for less than 30% of *James Beard Award* Chef finalists, 33% of *Food & Wine's* Best New Chefs, and 0% of the *World's 50 Best* (Kludt). Given that women and minorities are so prevalent in food media, why are they so underrepresented in these categories? Michael Ruhlman, examining race, and Charlotte Druckman, examining gender, both concur from interviews with chefs that mentorship plays a significant role in a young professional's success. Milton Guzman has observed that young black chefs entering the kitchen are finding few mentors willing to guide and support them (qtd. in Ruhlman). Similarly, Ann Cashion argues in "Skirt Steak" that for young women who lack an influential mentor, working together is the best way to help each other get ahead (qtd. in Druckman "Skirt Steak" Kindle Location 1008). If who you know determines how far you'll go, for female, non-white, lower-class chefs who do not see themselves reflected back in a peer group, breaking into the industry becomes much more difficult.

As the #MeToo movement goes forward, a radical, intersectional feminist approach must be employed in the professional kitchen. *Time's Up* for Batali, Hallowell, Besh, and all of the abusers who came before them. As labor is devalued on the basis of race and gender, a culture of violence and sexual aggression must be what is pushed out of the kitchen, not expectant mothers, young women, or minorities. We need more Samuelssons, more Waters, more inclusivity and representation in the industry.

Works Cited

Aita, Nicole. Personal Interview. 16 December 2018.

Black, Rachel. "Gastronomie, Inegalité, Fraternité." *Anthropology News Website*, (2018), DOI: 10.1111/AN.858. Accessed 27 November 2018.

Cohen, Amanda. "I've Worked in Food for 20 Years. Now You Finally Care About Female Chefs?" Esquire, *Hearst Digital Media*, 6 Nov. 2017, https://www.esquire.com/food-drink/restaurants/a13134079/sexual-harassment-sexism-food-industry/.

Crenn, Dominique. "Photograph of San Pellegrino's 'Best Female Chef' Jury." *Instagram*, 5 Sept. 2017, https://www.instagram.com/p/BYrTNDBnpKE/?utm_source=ig_embed.

"Demographic Trends Illustrate Importance of Foreign-Born Workers." *The National Restaurant Association*, 14 Feb. 2017, https://www.restaurant.org/News-Research/News/Demographic-trends-illustrate-importance-of-foreig.

Druckman, Charlotte. Skirt Steak: Women Chefs on Standing the Heat and Staying in the Kitchen. San Francisco, Chronicle Books, 2012. Kindle Edition.

---. "Why Are There No Great Women Chefs?" *Gastronomica*, 10: 1 (2010), 24–31, DOI:10.1525/gfc.2010.10.1.24. Accessed 18 November 2018.

Galarza, Daniela. "Restaurant Workers File More Sexual Harassment Claims Than Employees of Any Other Industry." Eater, *Vox Media*, 7 Dec. 2017, https://www.eater.com/2017/12/7/16746064/sexual-harassment-restaurant-workers-data-servers-cooks-bartenders.

Haddaji, Majd et al. "Women Chefs' Access Barriers to Michelin Stars: A Case-Study Based Approach." *The Journal of Culinary Science and Technology*, vol. 15, no. 4, 17 Sept. 2016, https://doi.org/10.1080/15428052.2017.1289133.

Harris, Deborah. Taking the Heat: Women Chefs and Gender Inequality in the Professional Kitchen. New Brunswick, Rutgers University Press, 2015. Kindle Edition.

"Hospitality Employee Turnover Rate Edged Higher in 2016." *The National Restaurant Association*, 16 Mar. 2017, https://www.restaurant.org/News-Research/News/Hospitality-employee-turnover-rate-edged-higher-in.

"John Besh Restaurants Fostered Culture of Sexual Harassment, 25 Women Say." New Orleans Business News, *Advance Local Media LLC.*, 21 Oct. 2017, https://www.nola.com/business/index.ssf/2017/10/john_besh_restaurants_fostered.html.

Johnson, Stefanie & Madera, Juan. "Sexual Harassment Is Pervasive in the Restaurant Industry. Here's What Needs to Change." *The Harvard Business Review*, 18 Jan. 2018, https://hbr.org/2018/01/sexual-harassment-is-pervasive-in-the-restaurant-industry-heres-what-needs-to-change.

Judkis, Maura & Heil, Emily. "Rape in the Storage Room. Groping at the Bar. Why is the Restaurant Industry So Terrible for Women?" *The Washington Post*, 17 Nov. 2017, https://www.washingtonpost.com/lifestyle/food/rape-in-the-storage-room-groping-at-the-bar-why-is-the-restaurant-industry-so-terrible-for-women/2017/11/17/54a1d0f2-c993-11e7-b0cf-7689a9f2d84e_story.html?utm_term=.b552a6f9529a.

Kludt, Amanda. "28 Pie Charts That Show Female Representation in Food." Eater, *Vox Media*, 20 Nov. 2017, https://www.eater.com/2017/11/20/16595308/female-women-representation-in-food.

"Leah Chase: National Visionary." *The National Visionary Leadership Project*, http://www.visionaryproject.org/chaseleah/.

Matwick, Kelsi. "Language and Gender in Female Celebrity Chef Cookbooks: Cooking to Show Care for the Family and for the Self." *Critical Discourse Studies*, 14:5 (2017), 532-547, DOI: 10.1080/17405904.2017.1309326. Accessed 18 November 2018.

McCarron, Meghan. "When Male Chefs Fear the Specter of 'Women's Work.'" *Eater*, 30 Nov. 2017, https://www.eater.com/2017/11/30/16687914/toxic-masculinity-restaurants.

Moskin, Julia. "A Change in the Kitchen." *The New York Times Company*, 21 Jan. 2014, https://www.nytimes.com/2014/01/22/dining/a-change-in-the-kitchen.html.

Pershan, Caleb. "Dominique Crenn, San Pellegrino's 'Best Female Chef,' Calls Out Company For (Latest) Gender Bias." Eater, *Vox Media*, 6 Sept. 2017, https://sf.eater.com/2017/9/6/16263038/dominique-crenn-san-pellegrino-gender-bias

Raphelson, Samantha. "Allegations Against Celebrity Chefs Reveal Abuse in the Restaurant Industry." The Salt, *NPR*, 14 Dec. 2017, https://www.npr.org/sections/thesalt/2017/12/14/570863486/allegations-against-celebrity-chefs-reveal-abuse-in-the-restaurant-industry.

Ruhlman, Michael. "Black Chefs' Struggle for the Top." *The New York Times Company*, 5 Apr. 2006, https://www.nytimes.com/2006/04/05/dining/black-chefs-struggle-for-the-top.html.

Samuelsson, Marcus. *Yes, Chef*. Random House, 2012. Kindle Edition.

"The Glass Floor: Sexual Harassment in the Restaurant Industry." Restaurant Opportunities Center United, *ROCUNITED*, 7 Oct. 2014. http://rocunited.org/2014/10/new-report-the-glass-floor-sexual-harassment-in-the-restaurant-industry/

Tuder, Stefanie. "Michelin 'Can't Do Anything' to Change Lack of Female Representation, Director Says." *Eater New York*, 31 Oct. 2017, https://ny.eater.com/2017/10/31/16585764/michelin-diversity-panel-women-chefs.

Valenti, Jessica. "To Eliminate Sexism from the Kitchen, Women Chefs Just Start Their Own." *The Guardian*, 15 Jan. 2015, https://www.theguardian.com/commentisfree/2015/jan/15/eliminate-sexism-kitchen-women- chefs-start-their-own

Zorn, Sarah. "Women Dominate Food Media, So Where Are the Stories About Female Chefs?" Shondaland.com, *Hearst Young Women's Network*, 7 Dec. 2017, https://www.shondaland.com/inspire/a14302416/how-food-media-should-better-cover-female-chefs/.

www.ingramcontent.com/pod-product-compliance
Lightning Source LLC
Chambersburg PA
CBHW070041030726
47506CB00003B/820